BUT!! YOU SAID, "I LOVE YOU"

THERE IS HEALING IN MY BROKENNESS

BY TAKEYA DAVIS

ISBN: 978-1-7943-9489-6

Contents

I would like to dedicate this book, "But!! You Said, "I Love You"" to my three awesome and wonderful children DeAndre, Kaniya, and Trinity. I love all three of them dearly with all my heart, and there is nothing in this world I would not do for them. Becoming their mother has taught me the definition of unconditional love and what sacrifice is all about. I would also love to dedicate this book to my grandson Carter. I have been blessed with this handsome bundle of Joy that melts my soul. It is such a blessing to become a Glam-Ma (Grandma). He has brought so much joy to my heart.

To my mom, Linda and Grandmother Mary, thank you for raising me to be an intelligent, smart, independent woman. Someone that will never give up no matter how much I wanted to. My loving sister Kisha, I've called on you at times when no one else was there, and you came right away in the nick of time. My bothers Tyrone and Jequante, how could I leave you out? I have unpaid bodyguards, thinking they are my dads.

Last but not least, my father, Herman. Who has showed no matter what life may throw at you, he will still be happy and wear a smile.

I love each, and every one of you and everyone I have mention has taught me something in life big or small. Family over everything.

Introduction

There comes a time in everyone's life where we may make the wrong decisions and detour to the right or left instead of moving straight ahead on the right path. Many times there have been roadblocks in the way, but eventually, you get through it. We have all been there, being in a harmful or toxic relationship. A relationship, we should have walked away from years ago before we actually did. Most of the time I got in my own way and ignored the warning signs or red flags to get out and move on. Not wanting to start over in a relationship again. Many people are in your life for a season, but some of us refuse to know when the story is over. Refusing to walk away caused me many of times losing myself trying to please other people. Eventually, I was at the point of brokenness. A place I refuse to go back to ever again.

When love hurts, it is time to walk away. I became addicted to pain in my relationships, refusing to walk away. It was a vicious and resolving cycle until God said, "No More." My experiences in life have made me the person I am today. God has the power to heal and deliver you through your brokenness.

CHAPTER 1

Growing Up In The Country

Country living has taught the real values of life because many things achieved, you really have learned to appreciate. I am from a small town called St. George, SC with a population of about 2,200 people. Everyone in the town knows each other and most call each other cousins. If you ask me, everyone is related so be careful who you date and get involved with. That person just may be your family member. Growing up in the country, you could stay outside until the street lights came on. Then you better be in the house, no excuses. These were the good ole days where the game Red Light, Green Light, 1,2,3 was the bomb, Double Dutching, or looking out the window playing, That's My Car. Real exciting games were played, and we really enjoyed them back in the day.

Most of the time my sister, Kisha and I were at my grandmother house in St. George because my parents worked so much and we caught the school bus from there. My grandmother Mary didn't play any games at all we were in church every Sunday and Wednesday night. Also bible study on Monday nights. On Saturday mornings when she hit the floor, everyone in the house was required to wake up as early as 5:30 am to get our day started. My sister, Kisha and I were required to help my grandmother in her gardens, which were more like fields instead of a basic garden that you find in someone's backyard. Everything was planted in the gardens such as green beans, sugar cane, squash, cucumbers, tomatoes, green peanuts, strawberries, corn, and butter beans. I'm missing a few things, but this is an idea of why we were required to get up so early before it became scorching hot outside. Many of times I would duck and hide when some of our friends and their parents drove across the railroad track going to town because I never wanted my friends to see my sister and I work in the garden, how embarrassing is that.

I will never forget in the winter times my grandmother had this huge wood fire heater that sat in the den area. This heater required wood logs from a tree to keep the fire burning. We were required to help stack the wood logs by the outside back door. When it was time, before nightfall everyone had to bring a few logs inside to make sure there was enough to cover through the rest of the night. The fire heater was huge and even scarier when required to open the iron door of the heater to throw the logs inside. Once the fire was lit and pumping this heater warmed the entire house. All you could see was smoke blaring out of the chimney.

My grandmother had a few kerosene heaters as well, and she kept one in the bathroom to make sure everyone stayed warm. Her car always smelled of gas because she would go to town and fill those little cans to make sure there was still enough for the heaters. One of the most frightening times of my life was trying to light one of those things. I was in the bathroom one night preparing to take a shower, but before then the heater had to be lit, so the bathroom was warm. While lighting this heater, my head was down and all of a sudden there were flames. The whole front of my hair was on fire. Yelling and screaming calling for my grandmother and sister

2

to come save my life. With a hair full of Blue Magic grease, you can imagine it was not easy putting the flames out. I bent over to the bathroom sink, and the flames were put out. My hair in the front was gone. Instead of wearing a regular bang in my hair, I had to start my bang part from the middle of my head and brush forward because the middle front portion of my hair was gone. This was in the 80's, and still, to this day I get laughed at by my sister Kisha, because who wears a bang in their hair, where the part begins from the middle of your head. I lost all my cool points for a few months during this time.

If you have ever lived or visit the country back in the 80's and 90's there were a lot of dirt roads, you have to drive miles and miles just to get to the city or even the mall for that matter. The great thing is I started learning how to drive at the age of 8 by sitting on my grandmother lap. Every chance she got, my grandmother was teaching us how to drive by the age of 10 and my sister was 12 we would take my grandmother car, drive to our friend's house that lived on a dirt road behind us. Sometimes we would drive to town to the grocery store or McDonald's. St. George is so small there are only about 2 red lights that I can think of, could be a possibility of 4 red lights at the max. Imagine given the car at the age of 10 and 12 driving anywhere you wanted to in town or across town, never getting pulled over by the police, smart enough to make sure we are driving the speed limit.

Not only did I learn how to drive at an early age but we were taught to be self-sufficient, so I learned how to cook as well. Can you imagine seasoning and frying chicken at that age in the kitch-en, making green beans from grandma garden and some rice to go with it? By the time I was 12 I was cooking just about any and everything. The town was small, so everyone knew each other, and we were very popular in school because my parents were well known. Everyone knew my grandmother as well. They all knew Mary that lived across the railroad tracks with the beautiful gardens or fields.

My parents had a trailer in a small town called Bowman, Sc. When we were at home from school, my mom or dad would drop us off at my dad parents' house in Shady Grove, SC. This is another small community to catch the bus with my auntie Cookie, my dad sister. They were in the same school district as my grandma Mary. Living in a small town, my aunt Cookie could park the school bus in my grandparent's yard, and we would leave with her for school in the mornings. How cool and awesome was that to leave the house on the school bus your Auntie drives? This is just how small the community was. In the Country, this will show you how different it is in the city. Living in the city does not allow you to drive your school bus home for the next workday. It just shows the difference between the country living and the city. My dad side of the family is well known also, so that made my sister and I even more popular. My sister and I were known as and still known as Linda and Herman (Toot) daughters.

In our backyard, there was a pig pin because my dad raised pigs. I can imagine him now running around the pig pin trying to catch them. This vision is quite funny. My dad would raise the pigs then sell them, as many other families did and still does in that area. Also in our backyard was our outhouse where my sister and I played with our pet rabbits. For some reason, we were in love with them.

CHAPTER 2

The Devastating News That Changed My Life

How can I ever forget the day we were told my parents were getting a divorce? I cried and cried until I was completely numb. I could not fathom my parents not being together and being separated from my father, he was my world. My dad Herman was a truck driver, we didn't see him much but when we did every time he blew the horn outside which means daddy's home. My sister and I would go running screaming, "daddy's home." If there were short trips, my dad would take us with him, riding in the big eighteen-wheeler truck flying down the interstate made our day. All we cared is that we're with our dad. Those memories, I would never forget. My mom decided to move to Orlando Florida. I begged my mother to stay with my grandmother because my sister and I didn't want to leave. Why leave? We were too popular in school. I could not imagine leaving all my friends and family behind because, at the age of 11, the country life was all I knew. There is nothing more I want to do but stay here with all my friends and family.

Mom left and moved to Orlando, Fl. to stay with some of our family members for two years to get herself together. My dad decided to move further up north, Brooklyn, New York. My mother was able to transfer her post office job to Orlando as well. She made a promise to us to give her time to get herself together then she would send for us. At that time I was not feeling it at all because I did not want to leave my grandmother, let along the rest of my friends and family. So for two whole exciting long years, my sister and I were able to stay with my grandmother. She was strict, as I don't know what, but hey that's what we were used to. Grandma didn't play the radio at all. Staying just made us more responsible as adults, but allowed us to stay with our friends and family, which was most important.

For two extra years, my sister and I were able to stay with my grandmother; all I really cared about was making sure we were still with our family and friends. My mother always reminded me that one day she will come back for us. At the time, I was not worried because two years seem a long time away. I kept asking if we could stay and continue going to school in South Carolina but of course, her answer was always the same, no and no again.

The time has come, the summer of 1989. My mother is on her way to pick us up from grandma house. Imagine me having to hug my friends on the last day of school telling them I'm moving to Orlando, Florida. Leaving everything I knew, going into the unknown. I was crying so sad, the hurt was unreal. Knowing I could come back for the summer seems far, far, away. Even though it was time to leave I was still begging my mother to please let me stay. Who would want to move to another state having to make friends all over again? I don't care about meeting new friends; I prefer to keep the ones I have, my mentality at the age of eleven. This summer we had to leave with mom and get familiar with the area where she purchased a home. On the way you could hear a pin drop, that is just how quiet it was in the car on the way to Orlando, Mickey Mouse World is what they call it. The whole summer I mainly stayed in the house, watched television and walked to the corner store for snacks. This was all the excitement my sister and mom could get out of me because I just don't want to be here. Most of the time I was locked in my room talking on the phone with friends I left behind.

The summer is finally over and the first day of school is here, sixth grade here I come going to middle school. Entering the world of the unknown was extremely hard, but I got through it, I guess. Sometimes at school, I would break down crying because I miss my dad so much. Getting off the school bus, not wanting to talk to anyone in the mornings, because thinking about how drastically my life changed within a short period of time. Being very heartbroken and devastated I didn't really care at the moment if I met new friends or not. This was really the last thing on my mind, new friends. Even though I was not the happiest camper day by day, it got more comfortable and more natural for me. New friends came along, and I was starting to become settled, I guess. Every now and then my dad would call, which brought me back to reality again.

It was a while before my mom started the dating scene, but when she did, I didn't have any understanding of anyone else coming around. The devastation of my parents' divorce literally tore me to pieces. When my mom brought people around, I would ignore them, and I would not talk to them at all. My sister and mom would say, I shouldn't be this way toward people, but this was something I just didn't want to deal with. There was no understanding from me what so ever the separation of my parents. A part of me was torn and by not talking to them, running them off was my way of saying, you're not welcome here. I'm sure there was many different ways this could have been handled, but back then I was young and wanted my parents back together. At my age when they separated at 9 all I knew was my dad. I was a true daddy's girl.

After a couple years, my mom entered into a relationship with Mr. James, he tried everything he could for me to like him, but I could not grasp the fact of him taking the place of my father. I can never forget Mr. James came to our house to introduce himself and I went into the room and closed the door. Saying to myself, "This can't be real," like "Mr. Who are you." He would take us out to dinner, and I would sit at the table the entire time and not talk. This is just how irrelevant he was to me.

My sister Kisha and I always laughed and made jokes about his car, "the shoe" is what we called it. The car was like a 1980 Chevrolet El Camino. Every time I saw this car we would laugh and sometimes laugh to the point with tears in our eyes. My sister was involved to, she wasn't always an angel. As time went by things for me would get a little easier. I was not as mean and bitter as I was in the beginning. Mr. James would invite us to his church, on some Sundays we would go out to eat afterwards. Even though I wasn't as mean I still kept my distant and didn't say too much. The relationship went on for about 3 years and eventually my mom and Mr. James decided to go their separate ways.

CHAPTER 3

My First Love

My mom found a Church on the West side of Orlando. We would commute about thirty minutes there and thirty minutes back on Sunday's, sometimes Wednesday nights. Who would have ever thought there was such a cutie in the building that played the keyboard and sometimes the drums by the name of Michael? Michael was really tall and handsome. What I really loved about him was that his family was an upcoming gospel-singing group. Michael's brother Charles had his eyes on my sister Kisha. We all were able to exchange phone numbers, and it was on from there.

Michael and I talked on the phone for hours at a time. Back then there was either a pager or house phone. The cell phone was the big block back then, and the only way to have one of those is if you were someone significant with a lot of money. Not too many folks could afford a cell phone at the time. Michael's parents were very strict so most of the time seeing each other at church and talking on the house phone was all we could do. I was in the seventh grade, and Michael was in the tenth, living on opposite sides of town. As time went along sometimes our parents would allow all of us to go to the movies or see each other outside of the church. My sister and I would learn to catch the city bus on Michael side of town, and we would all meet up in the downtown Orlando area, including his brother Charles and his cousin Doug. Doug had a crush on my cousin Jennifer so sometimes she would come along to meet up with him. All of our parents thought it was ok because again we all went to the same church together, including Jennifer. Sometimes it was without our parents knowing about it. At this age 13, I thought I was in love, of course, puppy love but I didn't see the difference.

Our hangout group became larger which included an adult by the name of Shay. She was the oldest out of all of us, at the time about 27 years old. I know what you're thinking, why would a 27-year-old want to be around 13, 15, and 17-year-olds? She was very heavy set and didn't really have a life at all. The parents were not really concerned for some reason, she was well trusted. So now we have Shay in the group, and everyone believed in and trusted in her because Shay attended our church as well. This made it easier for all of us to maneuver around and hang out because the excuse we used was, I'm with Shay, and she had our back. Shay drove a minivan and would come to pick us up from home then we would head to the opposite side of town to pick up the rest of the crew. This was perfect for all of us, no more waiting hours to catch the city bus, we would just call Shay. She would take us to pick up the other crew, sometimes go to the movies, downtown exchange, or even go back to her mother's house just to hang out.

About a year or so had passed, I'm home relaxing, and the house phone rings. It was Doug on the phone. Doug, the love of my life cousin is on the phone saying he needed to talk to me about something. I asked, Doug what is it? He said, "Takeya, Michael has been holding out on you about something that is going to break your heart." I said, "Michael wouldn't do anything to hurt me what are you talking about Doug?" As Doug started talking, tears began to roll down my face, the conversation was fading in and out because of what Doug was telling me. Doug said, "Takeya, Michael has been cheating on you with Shay, she has been sleeping with him!!!!!" (Blank Stare), What! Michael has been cheating on me with Shay? You mean to tell me, the Shay we trusted, the 27-year-old Shay is sleeping with my man, 17-year-old Michael? I don't believe you, Doug, that's impossible, why would you call me with this? I trusted Shay, why would she do this to me? This can't be real. Doug advised they had been sleeping together for a while and I should know because I was a great person and didn't want to see me hurt. My whole heart was crushed. I just knew Michael and myself had such a special bond, how would he allow Shay to do something like this? It just didn't make sense to me. I blamed Shay for everything because she knew all about my relationship with Michael. Shay was with us all the time, she was considered the adult watching over us, at least our parents thought.

Now my mom is involved, she came into the room asking what was going on? I'm at the point, I'm streaming! Mom, Doug is telling me Michael and Shay are sleeping together. My mom was like what? This can't be true. Once we got off the phone with Doug, my mom said, "We don't know the truth, let's talk to Michael and Shay first to see what is going on."

We all decided to go to Pizza Hut to meet up with Shay. Why we choose Pizza Hut, I don't know. Nothing has been confirmed as of yet, my mom wanted to speak to her first. We are all sitting around the table eating, and the subject comes up. Shay, I don't mean any harm, but we received a phone call today about you and Michael. Please tell me it's not true. Shay looked astonished and amazed, "what are you talking about"? My mom said, "There was a phone call today that you and Michael are sleeping together," please tell me it's not true. Shay drops her head, says "I can't believe this I would never do that, it's embarrassing." Believe it or not, we sat and ate after all the silence and tense was at the table. My mom was not buying it so she asked Shay, "Can I pick you up tomorrow"? We are going to Michael's parents' home to get to the bottom of this. Shay said, "It was ok."

My mom picks up Shay the next morning from her mother house, I'm sitting in the back seat heartbroken, upset, confused, emotionally devastated, and resentful. Shay is seated in the front of the Montero Sport, my sister and I are sitting in the back seat, on our way to Michael parents' house. We all walk upstairs into the parent's apartment, sitting around the kitchen table. Michael mom, Shirley begins to speak, saying "I'm not sure what is going on, but we have to get to the bottom of this. By this time everyone else is silent, not saying much at all. Shirley asked, "Who wants to speak first?" No one says anything, so Shirley was like, "Michael, please tell me why everyone is here?" Michael took a deep breath and said, "Shay has been pressuring me to sleep with her." "I'm sorry Keya, I'm really sorry for what has happened." Replying to Michael, "But, you said, I love you." How could you do this to me?" The tears began to roll down my face. The only thing I wanted to do at this point was jump across the table, slapping the shit out of Shay and Michael. Number one for the both of them making me feel and look so stupid and number two for lying this whole time, even when my mom confronted her. This entire time we put our trust in Shay because she was older than all of us, we looked up to her, and she attended our church, no wonder she didn't mind spending time with us, she was sleeping with Michael behind my back.

The tears kept rolling and rolling. The only thing I could hear was Michael mom Shirley apologizing to me, she was sorry this happened. At this point Shay was across the table looking like a ghost, I was furious. Michael's dad, Johnny was sitting at the table. Also, he apologized as well. Shirley was upset at the fact this happened because she saw my sister and me as her own daughters even though I was dating her son. She just kept apologizing and apologizing but what could we do now? What was done is done. I didn't have anything else to say. Removing myself from the table, waiting for my mother, sister, and Shay by the door. Shay rode with us to Michael parents' house, so she had to ride back with us to get dropped off. That was the longest ride of my life. Can you imagine finding out someone has been sleeping with your 17-year-old boyfriend and now have to ride in the same vehicle to drop her off at her mother home? Furious and frustration was an understatement. Shay got dropped off, and that was it for all of us with her. About 8 years later I saw her at a nail shop here in Orlando. She looked at me, I looked at her and kept it moving, haven't seen her since.

CHAPTER 4

Oh My God, I'm Pregnant!

I'm at work one-day taking orders at the front counter, yes working still at McDonald's. In walks a group of guys, I think it was four of them standing at the register making me feel some type of way. I realized out of the four of them there was one that had a lot to say. Don't get me wrong he was a dark skin brother, to top it off with a baldhead. I know you're asking, what I know about a baldhead brother at the age of sixteen? Well my answer is, not too much at that time, but I knew I liked what I saw, that's all, but didn't say anything. Ok, so back to taking orders! Welcome to McDonald's how may I help you? They all placed their order and asked for it to go.

Before leaving the counter, the baldhead brother introduced himself. Hi, my name is Edward, but many call me E. I responded, "Hi E, I'm Takeya, but call me Keya. Edward explained he just moved to Orlando from Cocoa, Florida to go to school at Valencia College. The question came up as to if I had a boyfriend. I advised no, then he asked me for my phone number and pager number, yes pager, LOL, we held a small conversation until my next customer walked up. There was a promised to call me later, and he left.

Later that night the house phone ring, it's Edward. We would talk on the phone for hours and hours. He told me his parents still lived in Cocoa, Florida but they sent him here to go to school. From what he was telling me his parents were well known in the community and well off. Edward didn't really need for anything. His parents got him an apartment and everything here in Orlando. Too bad my mom was strict and didn't allow me to go out on dates. If we were in a group that was different but I couldn't go with Edward alone at sixteen. Edward would come to my house every day, we were getting closer and closer. We would talk and watch T.V. for hours until 12:00am, my mom said he had to leave at midnight, she was not playing.

As teenagers, we would always find a way around what our parents told us we could do and not do. So some nights I was sneaking out of the house. Edward would page me when he was outside, and I would come out of the window or the back door and leave it unlocked until he would bring me back home. My sister, Kisha had already moved out of the house, so sometimes I would tell my mother I was at my sister apartment, but really I was staying with Edward. One night someone rings his doorbell and the girl at the door was yelling so bad he slammed the door in her face. She kept knocking and knocking, I'm in the room lying down. So E, who is that? That was just my ex-girlfriend, Tasha. Oh! Ok, why is she ringing your doorbell? E was like I broke up with her, she drove all the way here from Cocoa trying to save the relationship, but I told her it's too late. Brushing it off, but something didn't sit right with me. One night we were coming back to his place, and the same girl jumps out of her car when we pulled up. Tasha runs up to the vehicle, Edward got out and asked her to stop doing this, you're making yourself look like a fool, I'm with Keya, and you need to move on Tasha. She kept trying to get to me, but E was not having it. Eventually, I guess she got the point, didn't have to worry about her anymore at least I thought.

We are four months into the relationship and guess what I am pregnant. Yes, pregnant at sixteen. Oh my God, I'm only in the 10th grade. I'm still a baby myself I have no idea what I have done to myself. The phone rings, it's Edward, please come over here now, feeling sick, paranoid, frustrated, and scared all at the same time. My God, my mother is going to kill me, how do I even tell her? This is insane. Edward comes over, and he could tell something was wrong. We sit in the living room, and I started crying, my mother was in the room, has no idea what was going on. E I'm pregnant! His response was, "you can't be, my parents didn't send me here to get anyone pregnant, they are going to kill me." This is what you have to say? You're going to sit here and say this after you got me pregnant, I can't believe you. That's not it, he then tells me he already has a baby, and his parents are going to cut him off financially because they didn't send him to Orlando to have another baby, only to go to school. First I'm crushed because all he could think about was his self at the moment and secondly E never told me he had another baby already. Guess who the baby mother was? Tasha! Edward never mentioned a baby. This is why Tasha was going so crazy because he was lying to both of us. I needed him to help me figure all this out, I couldn't do this without him being right by my side.

Edward ended up leaving, he said we have to figure this out, and he left. I went to my room and closed the door, crying my eyeballs out. It took me about a week to get up enough courage to tell my mom what was going on with me. My mother and I didn't have a loving mother-daughter relationship or should I say not feeling comfortable to talk to her about it, I had no idea how I was going to approach her with this heartbreaking news. Come on at sixteen? I had no clue. One day I decided to write her a letter and explain everything to her in the letter because I was scared to approach her and let her know what was going on. The letter explained to her how I was feeling at the time and that I was pregnant. I packed a bag and left the note on the table after my mother left for work. I had no intentions of coming back home until things were cool and I knew my mother would be calm. I called Edward to come to pick me up, but I advised him if my mother called looking for me, to tell her he had no idea where I was.

A few days passed, and I decided it was time to return home. My mother met me at the door. She asked me to sit down at the table. I would never forget. She asked me how I expect to raise a baby. Do I understand how hard it is at my age to raise a child? I told her, I'm not sure how I will do this, but I will do it. That's all she had to say. I got up and went into my room. The only thing I could do was research and try to find a doctor. Everything I did on my own with scheduling a doctor appointment. I found a medical clinic for teen pregnancy, called and scheduled an appointment. At this point, I'm driving the Montero Sport passed down from my mother to my sister, then me. This Montero Sport was a brown box truck with no Air Conditioner. At the moment I couldn't complain because it was transportation to get me back and forth to school, work, and my doctor appointments. Can you imagine living in Florida and driving around with no Air Conditioner during the summer and pregnant, this was pure torture. The funny thing about it my sister Kisha drove us around in this box with all her friends included, with no shame what so ever, now it was my turn.

As long as the wheels were turning my friends were riding. They didn't care the truck was brown, shaped like a box and no AC, lol.

I kept asking Edward, "Have you talked to your parents yet?" "Did you tell them I am pregnant? Remember I haven't met his parents yet, we were a few months in the relationship. Edward kept saying his parents were going to kill him and he had no idea how he would talk to them about this. My mom was a little curious and started asking questions, asking "What does Edward parents think?" I didn't tell my mom what really was going on because she would be furious.

Edward began to distance himself from me. I realized he wasn't coming around that much anymore. When I would call he wouldn't answer or would answer with an excuse. Of course, my mom is asking a lot of questions again. Where is Edward? I would like to talk to his parents. We were trying to be nice about the situation at first but seem as though Edward was never going to tell his parents. My mother asked Edward for his parents' phone number. He was hesitant at first, but he gave it to her. When my mother called, there was no answer, so she left a message and asked for someone to call her back.

Ring, Ring, it is Edward mother, Brenda on the phone. My mom introduced herself and told Brenda I was Edward girlfriend and has Edward given her the news. Brenda was like, "What news?" My mother said, "Edward got Takeya pregnant, and I'm surprised he didn't tell you?" Brenda said, ooh that! Edward called me and said, "Takeya was pregnant, but he told me the baby is not his!" My mother literally almost dropped the phone. "What do you mean he is saying this baby is not his, he was at my house 24/7 and Edward is the only person my daughter was dating? My mother and Brenda exchanged a few more words and the line disconnected. At this point, I'm in tears. I was so devastated he would stoop this low and lie to his parents when I just knew he was in love with me. This explained the reasoning behind him distancing himself from me and barely coming around anymore because he knew he was lying to his parents. All this because they sent him to Orlando to go to school.

I'm calling Edward, no answer. Weeks and weeks passed and no call or visit from Edward. I couldn't believe this boy was putting me through this. At sixteen, I now realize I'm on my own with this pregnancy. The doctor appointments and everything was on me. I felt like there was not a support system. I'm all alone going to my doctor appointments and following up when needed. Still having to work and go to school as well. Crying became the norm for me, feeling emotional all the time. This was not all my fault, but I was willing to accept responsibility, what about Edward? How could he not have to take accountability for getting me pregnant? It is his fault as well as mine.

In the 11th grade, I'm walking around the high school campus with a huge baby belly. I couldn't feel more embarrassed, frustrated and disappointed that Edward was nowhere to support me through this at all. One day I decided to go to his job. At this time he was working for Sears. I walked in, and Edward was standing a few inches from the door as if he was the greeter for the day. I said, "Edward, why are you doing this to me? He ignored me like I wasn't there. After trying to talk to him for a few minutes, Edward asked me to leave before he gets fired. But you said, "I love you." I walked out in tears feeling like I was having an anxiety attack.

Later on that night I went to Edward apartment, and he wouldn't answer the door. His car was parked outside. Feeling so upset I went back to his car and kicked a massive dent on the side that bent the fender. Not only that, I wrote my initials on the hood of his car. Now, see what your parents have to say about that E. At this point, I just knew I was on my own through the rest of my pregnancy. I made sure to be at all my doctor visits, at school, and work on time.

One day I'm in the kitchen cooking some pork chops, green beans, and yellow rice. I ate once the food was done. After eating I was feeling a little weird and tightness in the stomach. The tightness turned into pains, I was having contractions and didn't even realize what was happening to me. The pains became worst and worst, now I'm yelling for my mom to come out of the room. I said, mom, I think I'm having contractions. I got my packed bag, and my mom rushed me to the hospital. Once I got to the hospital, I was in pain and feeling nausea. All the food I just ate came up, it was a mess.

On May 18, 1996, I had a beautiful baby boy by the name of DeAndre, was precisely a week early. He was 5 pounds and 14 ounces, 21 inches long. I was a mother at the age of 17, I could not believe it. I could not believe how I made it through this process feeling alone. My baby boy was here and still no sign of Edward. My mother did reach out to him and advised I had the baby. DeAndre was about 3 months before Edward saw him. At this point, I didn't have anything to say to him. He was such a disgrace to my baby and me at this point. The audacity of him to get me pregnant and leave with no remorse. To deny the fact I was pregnant by him, there were no words.

DeAndre came close to the end of my 11th grade school year, so due to my grades, I was able to pass and go to the 12Th grade. I had the whole summer to bond with my son before it was time to go back to school for my 12th grade school year. Motivation and determination is something that was instilled in me from an early age so going back to school was not a question at all. I knew I had to finish high school. My summer was busy because not only am I going to the doctor for my checkups, I'm also taking Dre back and forth for his check-ups as well. In our world, it was just him and me because my support system was the bare minimum. Due to me now having a little one I decided to go buy my very first car on my own. My mother already advised she would not cosign and I was on my own. It was ok for me to bare riding around with no air conditioner, but I didn't want my baby riding around in a hot car that was not going to happen.

My first car purchased was a Kia Sophia, a Kia in 1996. They were actually just coming out with the Sophia and I felt really good about my purchase. I did this on my own by putting a $1,000.00 down and purchasing my own insurance policy. My mom was not playing with us, we were taught to become responsible early. I had my Sophia for about a week, the air conditioner start making a loud clicking noise. This was a brand new car so why is the AC making this noise? I took it back to the dealership, they said whatever it was, and they fixed it. Less than a week later I'm riding down Colonial Drive, one of our main roads to the in and out of Orlando, Florida taking Dre to the doctor for his checkup, trying to stop at the red light and I have no brakes. I'm constantly pumping and pumping, the car would not stop. It was just me and Dre in the car, I was streaming, ooh God, the car won't stop. I put the car in neutral and eventually got it to stop, feeling so terrified. That was the last straw for me with this so-called brand new car. My mom and I ended up taking the car back to the dealership and demanded my money back but they refused. I had to get another car from the dealership and the deposit was transferred over to the new vehicle. The car I ended up with was a Mazda Protégé. To me it was better quality and looked like something I should be driving at the time.

CHAPTER 5

Senior Year In High School

Refusing to give up and not graduate on time, I went back to school finishing up my last year of high school. Every morning I would get DeAndre dressed first, then get myself dressed. Making sure I left the house in time to drop him off at the day care, then continue my journey to school every morning. Regardless if I was ready for the responsibility or not, there was no choice. I was beginning to see and feel what unconditional love was all about, just him and me in this vast world. Not only was I dropping Dre off at the daycare but after school went straight to work. I left McDonald's during the time I was pregnant and began working at Kentucky Fried Chicken. If there weren't anyone to pick Dre up from the daycare, I would go pick him up, drop him off at a friend house to babysit, then head to work. Talking about becoming a responsible young lady, I had no choice. Edward was missing in action so I couldn't depend on him for anything. Eventually, I put him on child support.

Everyone at school always asked about DeAndre. They remembered me from the previous year, 11th grade walking around with a pregnant belly. When I returned for my senior year many where surprised how I bounced back, like never skipping a beat. Always made good grades in school so graduating on time was not a concern. The only thing now that I look back on is missing my high school prom. At the time I just didn't want to go. Looking back now I wish I attended and had great pictures to look back on. Of course, because I was a young mother at the age of 17 caused me to miss out on a lot of events my friends were able to attend.

Its graduation time, the year went by so fast. I couldn't believe that I was about to walk across the stage with my high school class of 1997 with all my friends that saw me go through the ups and downs of my relationship and my pregnancy.

After the selfishness of Edward for almost a year, we began talking again. I know what you're thinking, how stupid could I be right? I was young and dumb for allowing him back into DeAndre, and I circle. Feeling really stupid I still allowed him in. Honestly, there were still feelings for him. Edward wanted to take myself and Dre to Daytona Beach for the weekend as my graduation gift. Asking my mom if it was ok to go point blank her answer was no. She said, "I could go but couldn't go for the weekend." At this point, I'm furious and upset. Why can't I go away for the weekend? It's my graduation gift, and Edward wants to stay the whole weekend. My point to her was, I already have a son by this man, why can't I go? You're not being fair mom, at all. This simple weekend getaway started an argument I didn't feel was really necessary. Yelling, I said, "I'm going anyways." My mother told me if I left to take all my belongings because I would need a place to stay.

Sitting in my room upset thinking what should my next move be. I went into the kitchen and got the largest trash bags I could find and started throwing all my clothes in them. My mother knew that I was strong-willed and if I left I would do everything possible not to come back. I called Edward, told him what was going on and if it was ok if DeAndre and I moved in with him. Even though Edward and I were having severe issues but trying to work things out, he was okay with it. Loading my car and crying at the same time because I knew this was it for me. The responsibility was already there because of my son but finally moving out of my mom house was huge. I was still 17 right out of high school, but refusing to allow my mother to tell me I still have a curfew of midnight when I have graduated from high school and have a full baby at home. All my stuff was loaded in the car and mom could not believe it, but she didn't say much at all. She knew there was nothing that could have been said to hold me back.

Living with Edward the first couple of months were fine. I was cooking because that's what I love to do, he didn't have a problem with it. But all of a sudden the tables turned. Edward was not coming home and would stay away for days. He never asked me to pay any bills, but I did buy grocery to cook, and of course, I kept my job. Edward again failed me. I honestly thought he changed but was I wrong. Sometimes I would be calling him on his phone, but there was no answer. Again I put my trust in him, and he failed me. During this time there were pagers. I would go use the pay phone and call one of my friends Trisha and talk for hours. Trisha was living with her boyfriend as well but going through some similar issues as me. Edward didn't have a phone at home, so I had no choice but to use the pay phone. My routine was the same Edward knew where I was. I would take Dre to the daycare, go to work and come home. Edward would not be there. Sometimes he wouldn't come back for days at a time. Here I was again I'm at the point where I needed him, and this is the return I get. Disappointed but not surprised.

My sister Kisha had her own place, and her lease was almost over. She knew everything that was going on with Edward and I. So ready to move I asked her if she wanted to get an apartment together because I was tired of living this way. How could Edward do me like this when I have his son and disrespecting me by not coming home? He was in for a rude awaking. My sister and I rented an apartment together. She paid half of the bills, and I paid half with a two-bedroom apartment. I eventually moved out without telling Edward I was leaving. What difference did it make? He was never there for us anyways. The money I made at the time was enough to share with a roommate but not on my own. We moved into our place, I was still working at KFC. My hustle was always on point, I had no choice, and all I knew was raising my son and working. We were settled in and here comes a pity sorry story from Edward. There was a change in him. All he wanted to do was be under me like he never had a life. This guy was always around at my place like he didn't have a place of his own. Damn Edward, now I feel like you're a leach on my neck. I couldn't go anywhere without him. Talking about being smothered. I just couldn't understand why now? Now that I have moved out on my own, well my sister and I, he wanted to act like he had some common sense and be in a relationship with me.

I'm at work one day, and this fine brother came walking in. I was working the front counter that day at KFC and took his order. When someone is looking at you like their checking you out, I couldn't help but start feeling a little nervous. After fixing the food coming back to the counter, collecting the money, he said,

"My name is Andrew what's yours?" "I said blushing; I'm Keya." He wanted to know if he could call me sometimes and I said yes. Yes, because there was all this confusion with Edward and I. It was time for some new friends.

Home from work, my room phone rings, and it was Andrew. Here I am blushing again just to be talking to someone different at least I thought. So here we are on the phone talking about where each of us are from, and Andrew tells me he is from the Titusville area which is not too far from Cocoa where Edward was from. We're both laughing and carrying on with the conversation, and I told him my son father is from that area. Of course, he wanted to know who and I wanted to see if he knew Edward or not. Andrew told me no. Our phone conversation ends about an hour later promising we would talk to each other soon.

Later on that night Edward comes over, noticing he was upset and really quiet. He comes into the room saying he needed to talk to me for a second. I'm like ok, what's up? Edward just starts going off saying I'm cheating on him and that Tasha, his ex, called him, and said, "I approached her boyfriend at KFC and gave him my phone number." I said, what the hell are you talking about? "Tasha said you tried talking to her boyfriend Andrew today." Me replying, "Andrew is Tasha boyfriend?" "What a small world it is." Edward said, "Andrew went back and told Tasha who I was and that I tried to talk to him." Basically, when Andrew found out, I was Edward son's mother he ran back to Tasha to cover himself before Tasha found out he was the one that approached me. Clearly, when I got off the phone with Andrew, I had no idea he knew Edward or Tasha. Little me, just thought the conversation ended and we would talk later. Andrew threw me under the bus to try and save his relationship with Tasha by saying I approached him first and that's what they told Edward. I said, "What a snake. Edward, Andrew is lying?" "I was taking his order at the register, and he asked me for my phone number." I just could not believe what the odds were of someone approaching me at KFC and its Tasha boyfriend. That snake was lying, and he knew it. Edward kept going on and on like he didn't believe anything I was saying. The whole story got turned around like I was such a cheater. We were in a serious argument, and I told Edward to leave. I couldn't believe this snake tried me like this to cover himself. So much for me deciding to give out my phone number. My relationship with Edward went downhill from that point, and honestly I was burnt out with him, so eventually, our relationship just ended.

CHAPTER 6

A Taste Of The Single Life

The single life to me at this point seems like the only way to go. I was free of the stress and drama. Something I have not experienced for a long time and I'm only 19 years old. Dre is two years old now. While at work some of my close friends would watch him or their parents who fell in love with him. Never had a problem finding a babysitter. I was always about my hustle. My money was needed because Dre and I had to eat. Working was not a problem for me. I could go out and party, only have an hour of sleep, then get up and go to work. Yes, these were the good ole days.

Started hanging out with some of my friends that I met in middle and high school. I was always the driver wherever we went. Just like back in the days when I was driving the Montero Sport with no AC, my friends didn't care as long as we were riding and getting to where we needed to be. We were hot, sweaty and all but still riding. There were a few clubs we would hang out at. One was called Club 436, which stayed open until 2:00am, and once we left there everyone would head to another club in Eatonville, Florida called Hero's Night Club. Hero's would remain open until 6:00am. After the club was over the crew would go to the Waffle House for breakfast sometimes not getting home until 9:00am the next morning. There was no way I was turning back to boring

Edward. He let me get a taste of the single life, and that was it for me. This was a repeating cycle every single weekend. The club was always jumping on Friday nights.

Even though I was only 19 people were offering drinks in the club, and no drinks were ever turned down. There would be drinks after drinks. It was so easy to get drinks in the club, and no one was walking around checking I.D. or anything. One night we were in the club partying like we never partied before and someone sprayed mace in the air. People were running and screaming trying to get out of the building. Some were trampling over each other trying to get out. This particular night it was just another friend and me when this happened instead of running towards the door we raced into the bathroom, coughing trying to get it out of our system. Everything calmed down, and the DJ's started playing the music again. My friend was like, "Takeya let's go." I was not ready to go. We ended up staying until the club closed at 6 in the morning.

It seems as though hanging out at the clubs and drinking alcohol became an essential part of my life. There was a temporary void that was being filled. First, my parents get a divorce, my first love cheats on me with an older woman, and Edward took me through a whole bunch of hell. All this and I was only nineteen. Always on the scene whenever there was an event, the crew and I was there. One night we were at the club, and the DJ said over the speaker, "They're towing cars out there you better go check to see if you parked in the towing zone." In my own lane tipsy as I don't know what I ignored the DJ, just knowing they were not talking to me. I'm a regular, I know where to park and not to park. My friends and I kept juking and dancing to the music, feeling great with no worries. It's 6:00am in the morning, the club closing, walking outside and no car. Damn, they towed my car. Standing outside looking crazy because the DJ warned us they were towing cars but we were so busy juking, I just knew my car was still outside. Trying to find out what company towed the car, someone yells out, "Such and such towed the cars but we just called, and they stated their office won't be opened until 9:00 am. The company started towing vehicles at 1:00am, so that means they already had my car for about 5 hours and have to wait at least 3 more hours before the office open. I ended up having to catch a ride home, and someone else took my friends home because we lived in two different directions. Eventually, I was able to get my car back for $275.00. This ended up being a costly night.

How can I forget the night of turning 21 years of age? I will always remember the party started at Club 436 at about 10:00pm and ended at 2:00am then heading on to Hero's Night Club to finish out the night. That night I could never forget. Everyone was buying me drinks after drinks, literally could not remember my name. Yes, not good at all. Always in the club turned up. Not only that the same night someone offered me weed for the first time. Of course, people were smoking in the club all the time. After the club, I'm driving to my sister and I new place. Some brand new apartments we decided to move to. Driving home, leaving the club, I see some blue lights flashing behind me. Pulled over in the Popeye's parking lot, the officer walks up to the car. At this point I am terrified. So scared that my high just left and no longer was I tipsy. The officer walked up to the car and said, "Ma'am are you ok?" "I followed you a couple blocks, and you were driving really slow and over the line a little." "I said, officer it's been a long day, I'm exhausted, today is my birthday, I'm 21."I worked all day then my friends wanted to take me out, so I haven't had any rest. Knowing I just smoked weed for the first time and was drinking. The officer said, "You look really tired, and your eyes are bloodshot red, are you sure you're ok and will be able to make it home?" I said yes, I'm not too far away I can make it. He asked for my registration and driver's license, did a check and let me go." Can you believe it? He let me go! I just knew I had to call my mom or sister to come to pick me up from the County jail.

At 21, Kentucky Fried Chicken became a part-time second job for me. My full-time employment was as a bank teller at "Washington Mutual, which is now Chase Bank." Even though I was a party head. I still took care of my business when it came to paying bills and being responsible. People would look at me like, oh she is so sweet and innocent not knowing that I truly lived a party life. I would go hang out all night Friday night until 6:00 in the morning and have to be at work some Saturdays at 8:30am. Hangover and all I was there, I had to support my lifestyle. But not only that I had a little one to take care of as well. My sister didn't mind babysitting because she had my niece Bri that was two years older than Dre.

One day my sister breaks the sad news that her boyfriend at the time, now her husband wants to move in and when the lease is up, they will be moving. It didn't bother me as much because now I'm 21 and can afford a place on my own. I decided to look for a house, at 21 considering buying a home. Doing some research, I found a program for first time homebuyers where they would offer $30,000.00 in down payment assistance. No idea what I was doing, I called the number, and a lady answered. Explaining to her what I wanted to do and she gave me a breakdown of the program. She advised of a neighborhood that was just being built up, but it was on the West side of Orlando. More like Pine Hills area. I'm thinking to myself I hang in that area anyway so this would be perfect for me. This would be a brand new home, I had to wait a few months to build. There was still time before our lease was up, so it didn't bother me at all.

During this time I'm working two jobs. One as a Bank Teller and my second job was still at KFC as a Shift Supervisor. Many of us that worked at KFC hung out together. One of the shift supervisors Shannon, that got transferred to our restaurant we became really close. So close when people saw us together, they would call us One Red, One Black. Shannon was dark skin, and I was light skin. That is where our names came from. Also my girl Mona, we went to school together and ended up working at KFC together. We hung out and did dirt together but ran KFC like a champ, we had it under control. Kentucky Fried Chicken was my splurge money. I had to be able to support my habit, which was buying a new outfit each time to go out and my party life. The bank check was for bills, so I definitely had a plan.

One night at Hero's Night Club the crew was having a great time. I'm standing beside Shannon, One Black and I see someone pulls her and whispers in her ears. The next thing I know, she looking at me smiling up a storm saying, "Justin wants to talk to you." He was standing on the side of Shannon waiting to see my response. I looked at him and was saying to myself, "wow he is really handsome and just how I like, dark skin and handsome." Shannon gave him the ok, and we started talking. He introduced himself, and I introduced myself. Justin advised he was originally from England. His parents moved to England after leaving Jamaica and eventually moved to Florida. Explaining to him, I was originally from South Carolina but have been here for years. He offered to buy me a drink, of course, I took him up on the offer, and we exchanged numbers and went back to our crew.

Even though Justin was 8 years older than me, he and I started spending more and more time together. He lived on the West side of Orlando in the same area I was getting my house built. Actually, the guy Shannon was talking to Toby, he and Justin were best friends and roommates living together. We were at their home all the time. I would pack little bag, Dre and me would stay with Justin on the weekends.

My home was being built, and there were about three more months before the closing date. In the meantime, little Dre and I were back and forth from my apartment with my sister to Justin house. Never forgetting the Lender gave me a closing date in April of 2000, and the home was not ready. My sister and I got into a huge argument because she wanted me out the apartment so her boyfriend could move in. We argued because the lease was not up yet, don't rush me to move when my house is not even ready. One day the argument got so heated I went and got a U-Haul truck packed all my belongings and left. Dre and I went to my mom house because I had another month or so before my home would be ready. Of course, when I left my mom house in 1997, my intentions were never to go back to stay. Making a promise to myself that I would never be back but my sister gave me no choice. Not only was I upset with my sister Kisha for making me leave the apartment when my home was not even ready. I was bothered with her for putting me in the situation to have to go back to mom's house when I made a promise to myself and my mom I won't be back to stay. Sounds stubborn right? Yes, it was a pride thing I guess. Basically showing all of them I'm a person of my word and I can survive and make it with my son. Even telling my mother, I was buying a house no one could believe it. They were trying to find out how was I going to do this with a son. I was a party animal, but common sense was nothing I had to worry about.

CHAPTER 7

My House Is Ready! It's Move-In Day

May 21, 2000, my house is ready to move in. Justin and I got a U-Haul truck loaded it up and was on our way. There was not too much to move because most of the furniture I purchased and was going to be delivered. There was a bedroom set my mom gave me, and I used that for the guest room. The set I had when living with my sister I put in Dre room and ordered a brand new bedroom set for my room. The home was a 3/2. My bedroom set was ordered from a local store, but shipping from overseas didn't get it until two months later. Everything was set up and delivered on time except for my bedroom set. Imagine being 21 years of age with a brand new home, working two jobs and a mother. I was about my business, but there was still a void in my life. Justin and I were getting closer and closer. He asked to move in, and I let him.

Not only did I move into my brand new home, three months later, but I also quit the bank and started a brand new job working for Bank One credit card division, which is now Chase. Making more money at Bank One but still holding on to KFC, working part-time. Living this life was fantastic at first even though Justin didn't have a car, I would let him drop me off at work and go hustle his money. Stop right there, I know you're saying, "How could you let him drop you off at work and take your car." LOL, I was in love ok! Ladies, don't act like you have never been in this situation before, where a man drop you off at work and take your car! When I think about Justin now, I think about the lyrics in the song by R&B artist TLC. "Riding On The Passenger Side Of My Best Friend Ride" LOL! Definitely can laugh about it now. Back then he was the CD man. Everyone knew Justin by selling great music. He would use a CD burner and make copies of music as people requested them. That was his hustle at the time. I was so in love, in the beginning, it didn't bother me. He was my chocolate fix, my chocolate drop, my Hersey Kisses, the love of my life. It didn't bother me until the bills started rolling around and Justin wouldn't have his share of the money. He was giving a $100 here and there but never his full half of the bills. This began to cause some chaos in our relationship. To the point, we would always be arguing about the bills around the 1st of the month. Justin would also pick up other jobs. He would DJ sometimes at clubs and parties, but those were rare. The arguments would start when I would tell him to please go get a job so you can make some guaranteed money to help pay these bills. Sometimes it would get to the point Justin was picking me up late from work. Questioning myself, why am I standing in the parking lot waiting for you to pick me up? When you have had my car all day. There should be no waiting time, I'm tired and worked all day. Of course, when I see my vehicle squealing on two wheels pulling up in the parking lot so fast because he knows he is late. Getting in the car with the expression on my face, "don't say a word right now until I calm down."

I loved this man dearly. He was one of the best dressers in the club. Well, one of the best dressers period. Where ever he went he was fresh and clean like there were no worries at all. The way he dressed, always new sneakers or suited up at the club, you would think he had his own car, house, a boat, a dog, a cat and a business. We would be in there like Bonnie and Clyde, and no one better say anything to my man. He is all mine. His family was really nice people, his mom, dad, and brother. We all had dinner together a few times just to relax and enjoy each other. Justin kids would come and stay with us for a couple weeks during the summer. His daughter lived in Michigan at the time, but his son was here in Orlando.

As time went by at the club, I would be so tipsy. So tipsy and drunk I couldn't remember what happened the next morning. Trying to get over a hangover the whole next day. Justin and I would have several arguments about the drinking. He would be drinking right along with me, but I guess he could hold his a little better than I could. One night at home we got into a heated argument about the bills and Justin left. He was gone for a few days, but I knew where to find him, and I knew once Friday hit he would be at Hero's Night Club. My crew and I walked in One Red and One Black, with some of the rest, just rocking to the beat and making our grand entrance, I see a VIP section roped off. As the club got full, I see Justin standing in the VIP section with One Black boyfriend Toby, his roommate and best friend. We didn't say anything at first because Justin and I are mad at each other and haven't talked for days about his share of the bills. Just to make sure we were seen, we walked by the VIP section. Justin knew at the time not to play with me, even though we were not on talking terms I considered him as still my man and don't mess with me.

Time goes by, and the club is full to its capacity. The DJ is bumping all of the greatest hits at that time. My radar goes off, and I see Justin standing up talking to this girl in VIP. Nobody knows but One Black, my ears are about to get hot, and my eyes are turning blood red. The next thing I know Justin is whispering something in her ear, and this is when I lost it. I walked up to the VIP rope, he saw me coming. Asking, "What the hell is going on"? I advised him I been watching him for a while and saw everything that happened. "Why are you trying to play me like this Justin?" He brushed me off like I was not talking to him. One Black knew how I was so she was trying to calm me down because the club was about to be shut down if he didn't stop acting a fool. We eventually walked off and went back to the dance floor. When the club was over by this time the whole crew was tipsy. We walked by Shannon car because she drove this time and waited for Justin to come outside with the rest of his crew. I will never forget Justin walked up to me and I swung on him then jumped on his back. We both fell to the ground and were wrestling in the grass where the car was parked, right outside the club. Eventually, they separated us, I got in the car with One Black, and Justin got in the car with his friend Toby.

The next week Justin and I were back together again. He told me all the time how much he loved me and I was soaking it up. The significant part about it was, he would take Dre with him a lot of times and even pick him up from the daycare for me because of my work schedule. Justin had some type of lawsuit that was settled, and out of those funds he was able to buy himself some transportation. I was doing flips on the inside because that meant no more having to drive my car. The car he had lasted for about 8 months, then here we go again, back to me being dropped off at work. I really feel that this made me more upset than anything. I'm tired of being dropped off so many of our arguments were about that.

Justin came home one day and said he didn't have to hustle the streets anymore selling CD's because he found a hair salon that would allow him to pay a small fee to set up a booth, so people know where to find him. I would always get on his case about finding a real job, but he would still say, "I don't believe in him." Everyone saw what I was saying but him. Since Justin is working at the Salon, I would drop him off sometimes on my way to work. Then pick him up on the way home. This all worked for a little while, but eventually, things really began getting heated. We could not see eye to eye for anything. There was always an argument about something.

There was a new spot for us to hang out at every first Friday located at Universal City Walk. Everyone looked forward to the first Friday of the month for this event. It was a dress to impress every time. This was our new place only on the first Friday. Justin made sure he was suited down and dressed to kill. Shannon and I used to go most of the time together sometimes with some of her cousins also. This place was the talk of Orlando back then. Eventually, my cousin Jennifer brought a house and moved to the same neighborhood as Justin and I lived in. One night the three of us decided to go out there and hang out. We were in my car, but Justin drove. On the way to the club, everything was cool, we were laughing and joking, playing around like we always do. When we got to the club, Justin went off with a friend of his, Jennifer and

I were hanging out. After a few hours past, we went looking for Justin to let him know we were ready to go.

On the way home, Justin asked if we wanted Waffle House. I said, "Yes." So while he was in Waffle House, I fell asleep in the car. When Justin got in the car, he was furious because I fell asleep. I mean he was yelling at me worst than a child. Justin was so mad until he was shaking. We are driving down Kirkman road, this man rolls the window down and throws the food out of the window on the highway. The next thing I know he drives a little further, pulls over in the median of the road, jumps out of the car and takes off walking, crossing the other side of the highway. My cousin and I look at each other like what is his problem. Jennifer jumped in the driver seat, and we drove a little until we could cross over to look for Justin as he walked to the gas station. Driving in the parking lot, I asked Justin to please get back in the car. He wouldn't do it. He yelled the only reason you fell asleep is because you are drunk. We were yelling back and forth, and I'm like you're acting like a fool, get in the car so we can go home. It was around 2:00am. He would not get in the car, so Jennifer and I left.

Jennifer went home, and I drove around the corner to my house. When I got home, I didn't call Justin. I lie in the middle of the bed and fell asleep lying on my back. Not caring how Justin would get home because he chose not to get in the car. I'm in a deep sleep and the next thing I know, there was water thrown in my face. I guess he decided to walk all the way home from where he got out of the car, which was about 6 miles away and all the anger and frustration built up on top of how mad he already was. When Justin got home, he went into the bathroom, filled the trashcan up with water and threw it in my face. I woke up out of a deep sleep swinging because I had no idea what just happened. When I woke up swinging, we were literally tearing my house apart. Furniture was broken, food that was on my kitchen table was all on the floor and on my ceiling. It was the craziest thing ever. I was so angry and upset that he didn't have any respect for me to throw water in my face from a dirty, nasty trashcan in the bathroom. It was his fault he decided to walk home.

So upset his CD burner machine was in the living room I picked it up and threw it outside of the front door. Knowing that was his moneymaker at that point I didn't care. He tried everything he could for me not to get to that machine because he knew that would be the end of that. When I threw the machine outside, he lost it and drug me out. I just knew that was it for me. Threating to call the police he left. By the time I called Jennifer, and she heard me crying, she and her mother came over immediately. Then they called my mother and sister. I was crying so bad I couldn't even talk to explain what happened. The police and I filed a report, Justin was long gone. A couple days later I dismissed the charges.

Waking up the next morning, not wanting to go to the hospital. My face was swollen with bruises on my face, legs, and arms. I looked a mess. Back then I had a piercing right above my lip. It was embarked in my skin from this incident I had to cut it out from the back of my upper lip with a razor. Looking at myself in the mirror I couldn't believe this happened. How can I possibly go to work looking like this? I couldn't! A week missed of work, but when I decided to go, so emotionally disturbed they sent me home for another week, and some of the bruises were still there. I could see the hurt in my manager's eyes that she felt for me. She told me not to worry to take the time I needed to heal.

After this happened I didn't see Justin for about a month. His dad came over to get his belongings and apologized to me for everything that happened. Now that he was completely moved out I was focusing on trying to get my life back on track. It wasn't easy because we were so used to Justin being around. We tried a couple times after this incident, but there were that hurt and void again. Trying to hold on to something just not meant to be. I will never forget one day sitting in church, the pastor called me out and said, "The guy you are with and trying to make the relationship work, is not for you." Immediately I knew that was confirmation from God to get out of that mess. I went home and cried until I couldn't cry anymore because I knew this was it. No more back and forth, we were done. Sitting in the house depressed and crying for a while. But I started thinking back on dreams I used to have when Justin and I were together. In the dream, there would be snakes falling out of my closet in a trash bag, a trash bag full of snakes. You know they say when you dream about snakes it means you have enemies that are close to you. And my question was, "Why would they be falling out of a trash bag coming from my closets?" Was God showing me I was sleeping with the enemy? Was Justin cheating on me? At that time I didn't understand. After Justin and I separated, we went our separate ways for good, the snakes in my dreams disappeared. At the ending of our relationship, I'm not sure if he was 100% faithful or not.

Even after the separation of Justin and I, he always gave me the music CD's still. We got along even better after time past and were no longer in that relationship. He eventually told me I help mold him into a better man because when I met him, we used to always argue about bills and finding stability. Justin said, "One thing about Keya she didn't play when it comes to taking care of responsibility." He thanked me for changing his whole perspective on responsibility. Not only was I molding him and didn't know it. But he saw me first hand, handling my business. I may have partied, and drunk alcohol but my responsibilities were always first. It felt wonderful for him to be able to recognize I was trying to help him for his good.

CHAPTER 8

Disappointed But Life Must Go On

S tressed and depressed with everything I had been through and was going through. I was drinking and cooking dinner one night. Everything was done except the green beans. Laying down on the couch I figured until the green beans were done. Within a quick second, I must have fallen asleep. Waking up to the smoke detectors, my house was full of smoke. I almost burned my whole house down, couldn't hardly breath. Thank God for the smoke detectors going off because I was in a deep sleep. When the smoke detectors finally woke me up, I couldn't hardly breathe or see because of the smoke. I immediately opened the doors and windows trying to let in some fresh air. I had to end up leaving my home, the smell was just that bad. Alcohol had become the norm for me to cover up the emotional pain in my life.

Finally, hearing from my dad brought back so many memories. My sister and I lost contact with him when he moved to New York. I was a daddy's girl. Not having him in my life even with what I had already gone through took a significant toll on my life. Finally, about 14 or 15 years of not seeing my dad, he decided to fly to Orlando. Such an incredible moment standing at the airport waiting to see my dad I haven't seen in years. Oh my, the tears that kept flowing were indescribable. My dad was my hero. I looked forward to him coming home in the big eighteen wheelers, honking the horn from down the road for my sister and me to go outside. Those were the good ole days that I still remember. A part of me was taken away or lost after this divorce. My dad could not believe that his baby girl was a homeowner at an early age and how great I was doing for myself and Dre. My sister was already married, and they were doing well also. My dad stayed with us for a week then flew back home.

Admitting I was still in love with Justin but knowing it was best to get out of it. It was the best for Dre and myself. Even though the relationship was toxic you feel like a part of you has died. I was still crazy about him that's the sad part but knowing God had spoken was the final say. Sometimes I would call in from work too depressed to go. My heart needed time to heal and didn't want to be at work feeling sad and depressed. Worrying had me stressed. Going through the process I lost about 20 pounds, not able to eat.

About 4 months past and I'm getting myself back on track. My workflow is back on track with Bank One and KFC. I couldn't stay down for too long because bills had to be paid. Even though there was all this drama in my life, I still had grown woman re-sponsibilities. Making sure Dre and myself were taken care of. Finally started to hang out again but it no longer was at Hero's Night Club or Club 436. Eventually, they were both shut down.

Jennifer, myself, and Jennifer god sister Nina started hanging out a lot more. Mainly we would go to the First Friday events and a few other spots, just a change of atmosphere. It was time. One Black would hang out with us as from time to time. Every year in Orlando there is an event called the Florida Classic. This event is an annual college football rivalry game between Bethune Cookman University and the Florida A&M University (FAMU U). People travel from all over the country just to be at this event. Friday night is the battle of the bands and the step show, also all type of parties to attend. Saturday during the day is the football game and different vendors at the Camp World Stadium in the downtown Orlando area. Saturday night is the primary night people would party the most because now we know who has won the game. Then there is Sunday. Sunday is always the car show. People come from all over just to participate in the car show on Sunday. We would start our Classic Weekend on Thursday nights and party through the whole weekend. On top of that my birthday falls between this weekend and Thanksgiving so because of this, I would have so much fun, and there would be so much excitement.

Sunday the crew and I decided to get dressed and hang out for the car show. We wouldn't go directly to the show, we would just be in the vicinity of the area. That's what many people did just to hang out. We're walking in crowds of people just parked, hanging out by their cars. Someone is yelling, trying to get my attention. How I knew he was talking to me is because I had on my favorite color, which was pink. I was pink from head to toe. This was my color, and I would rock it from time to time. This guy says, "My nephew saw all that pink coming, and he wants to talk to you, but he's really shy." So the crew stops, and we're all looking like what is this fool talking about? It was a group of them about 10 deep.

The nephew introduces himself, "Hi I'm Darius, my Uncle KJ is right I'm really shy, but I saw you coming and wanted to at least say hello, see if I can call you sometimes." At this point what do

I have to lose? My relationship with Justin is definitely over even though I'm still in love with him. Well, I gave Darius my number, the crew and I kept walking just hanging out trying to see what else was popping or going on. We stayed out in the area for a few more hours, it was time to go home. Our perfect weekend was wrapping up and coming to an end.

Before I could get home my phone rings, it's Darius! I'm saying to myself, "Can't be too shy he already calling." He was calling to see if we were hanging out that night. I advised him no, I'm on the way home, and I'm done hanging out for the weekend. It would be ok to come to see me in a couple days when I was off from my second job. Darius comes over, his car was a little old, but whatever at least he was riding and had a car to drive. Didn't have to worry about him asking me for my ride at all. I was free from those shenanigans. Darius and I began to spend more and more time together. He was really quiet. We would be sitting on the couch watching TV, and he wouldn't talk at all like he was a turtle in a shell.

Darius and I would have conversations about what we both wanted. I explained to him I was not having any more children until I got married. Really set on that because I didn't want to have any more children even when Justin and I were together. Mainly because of what Edward put me through. A couple months into our relationship Darius brought this huge floor model big screen TV. Back then this was a big deal. I think I mentioned to him I wanted a new TV in my living room and a few days later I had it. I was thrilled that this guy took it upon his self to buy this TV.

Four months into our relationship Darius ask me to marry him. Completely caught off guard I did tell him yes but not right now.

I couldn't marry him at the moment because at the time I was still in love with Justin, knowing he was not right for me. Marriage at the time was the last thing on my mind. Clubbing and partying was still on my mind so why would I want to get married? Darius wasn't the type to go out at all so when I was gone he would be at home with Dre and his son Quan, who he had custody of. Dre and Quan were two years apart. Dre was the oldest.

One day my phone rings, and it is Justin. He asked me if he could come over to talk I advised him no, not at the moment I have company at the house, it was not a good time. For some reason, he really wanted to talk to me so he asked if I could meet him down the street. A deep sigh! I said yes but only for a few minutes. Never forget, I met him down the road from my house in the McDonald's parking lot. Justin looked as though he was really serious. I'm looking at him like, "What's wrong with you?" Justin said, "I have been doing a lot of thinking, and I want my family back." Me, looking really shocked, knowing I had already moved on but was still in love with him. Juuusstin!!!! Why now? At that very moment, something inside of me said, "this is it…it's over you have to tell him." Teary eyes, looking Justin in the face I said, "Well Justin after our relationship ended I met someone, he asked me to marry him." His eyes started to tear up, we were both teary eyes, but deep down Justin was not right for me. The worst part was over after all the anxiety and depression I went through after our break up. I never wanted to feel anything like that ever again in my life. Justin gave me a hug, and we went our separate ways. Returning home explaining to Darius where I went, all he said was Oh! Ok! Is that all you have to say? Well, I'm okay with that, and we went on with our business.

CHAPTER 9

What? I'm Pregnant

Mad and angry with myself, I told Darius I would not have any more kids. The reason I felt this way is because of all the confusion and drama Edward put me through when I was pregnant with Dre and after the fact. I literally made a promise to myself no one would ever have the opportunity to take me through that again. Telling Darius, I was pregnant, at the moment I wasn't sure if he was happy or not. I knew I was crying because I wasn't really sure if I was ready to go back down this road again. Dre was already 8 years old when I got pregnant. Darius kept telling me everything would be ok. I know what you're saying, use protection and birth control. Yep, you're absolutely right. So we can't blame anyone. The only reason I was crying is because of what I already went through but at the same time, I was happy I'm having another baby. Me, getting pregnant with Darius happened about 5 months within our relationship. We were still getting to know each other but so far so good. Knowing I am pregnant, I was done with the alcohol.

When I told everyone I was pregnant, they couldn't believe it. Especially my mother and sister. They knew me and knew I was serious about what I said, "No more children until marriage." But of course, nothing worked out as planned. God had a purpose and plan, and it's not always our plan.

As the months rolled by I'm already pregnant and I find out Darius not only has his son Quan, but he is the father of 5 additional children. Yes, so a total of 6 kids plus mine that is on the way. Darius and I never had that conversation. He had me thinking Quan, which he had custody of was the only one until after I was pregnant we started mentioning the other children. There wasn't anything I had against children, I just didn't know. So as time went by he would bring his oldest two daughters with him and Quan to stay the night.

For a while we were doing really well. His family reminded me of my family. Very welcoming with open arms. I truly fell in love with his mother and grandmother. Both of them never played any games at all, but lovely women. Darius, the kids and I would go to church together, which was really a plus in my book. The church was important to me. Even though I wasn't living a perfect life, I knew God for myself, and anyone I dated went to church with me. Even Justin he went a few times as well when we were together.

February 9th, 2005, my daughter is here, Kaniya. At the beginning of Darius and I relationship, he was buying big screen TV's, rings, and giving money to pay bills all of a sudden things began to change. Was this just a front to swindle me in the relationship? Yes! Once my heart was into the relationship, things began to change. At this point every time Darius got mad, he would pack up his clothes and go back to his mother's house. Never forgetting one day, Kaniya, Dre, and myself went to church, came back to the house and my big screen T.V. was gone. Jumping on the phone calling Darius to see what his problem was there would be another argument and nothing would get accomplished, so the best thing to do was hang up. How could you possibly get mad and take the big screen T.V. back you gave me when we first met, that's so unreal.

About a year later, Kaniya was almost a year old I decided to sell my first home and purchase another home. This new home was a 4/2, a lot more space and with a pool. The area I was living in was not the best in Orlando. It was the Pine Hills area, known to many as Crime Hills. That says enough there. Pine Hills was also on the show First 48. Never forgetting this, one morning, leaving to take Dre to school, I was 8 ½ months pregnant with Kaniya. Leaving I would always come out of the house from the garage. When I lifted the garage, my car was sitting on bricks. Someone had to be watching my house because Darius would leave home the same time in the morning, about 5:00am. That same morning when he left, I walked him to the door to see him off to work and my car was fine. About 7:45am was when I came out of the garage to take Dre to school, I saw my rims and tires were gone. The worst thing of this all is the thieves dared to use my very own landscaping bricks from my yard to sit my car on. How sweet and considerate of them to do that? From that very day, I knew it was time for me to go. Of course, didn't want to make any changes while still pregnant so we were waiting for my Kaniya to get here. Before I had a chance to leave the neighborhood, there was a guy that held his girlfriend hostage in the car on our main road of the community and people were not allowed to leave their homes. This was all over the news. At this point, say no more God, I'm outta here.

When it was time to move Darius was no were to be found. I guess we were off that week and not talking to each other. He went back telling all his family I was moving and he couldn't understand why I wanted to move. I wanted to move because it was time for me to go. Not once did I ask Darius for anything towards the new home. This was something I got approved for on my own without the help of him. From day one I was always a go-getter, and he knew that. I just couldn't understand why he had a problem with it.

We were all packed up and moved into our new place. Not even a month from the time I moved in I received a call from a friend Corey saying, "can I come to get him? He needed a place to stay because his sister kicked him out of her house and there was no place for him to go. Really I didn't want to tell Corey no because he was the one that helped me move. By me having 4 bedrooms, I told him yes because there was an extra room. He understood he was required to pay rent. That was talked about when he asked if he could stay. I'm not sure what type of argument Corey and his sister had but that same night she drove over to my house and threw all his clothes on my lawn. How embarrassing was that? I'm new to the subdivision, and she came over and threw his clothes on the grass.

As soon as I moved in I started renovating the home, taking up all the carpet and putting down tiles and wood floors, changing out all the ceiling fans in all of the rooms, and of course the toilets in the bathrooms as well. Also, replace the front door with a glass door and the siding on the home. All the bedrooms were wood floors. There was absolutely no carpet in my house. Carpet didn't sit well with me. The handyman working on my home, as he pulled up the carpet, he laid it on the side of the road for trash. There was a knock at my door (doorbell ringing). Here was

a tall skinny white guy looking like a predator smoking a cigarette, flicking his buds, with a book in his hand. Immediately I'm
looking extra crazy because I despise the smell of cigarettes and
he had the audacity to flick the buds, standing at my doorstep.
The gentleman said, "I'm Nick, the next door neighbor. Have you
received one of these? Showing me the book!" I said no, what's
that? Nick said, "The Homeowner's Association Book" I repeat-
ed, "maybe but I just moved so it could be in the folder they gave
me." Nick said, "You're not supposed to sit this carpet on the side
of the road until the night before the trash truck comes." Me responding, "I'm renovating the home, and I have nowhere else to
put it, they can see I am redoing some things in the house. Nick
dared to blow smoke in my face. The only thing I remembered so
that I didn't go off on this man was to say ok and close the door.
From that day he didn't sit well with me.

There was my other neighbor on the right side of me, was
the coolest dude I ever met, Harold. Harold was the party guy on
the block, every weekend the cars would be lined up down our
street. Nick would sometimes call the police on Harold, saying
he always had traffic running in and out of his house. Harold son
Maine and Dre became best friends. Nick thought for some reason he was the neighborhood police. I could tell when he flicks
those buds on my front doorstep that day we were going to have
problems.

A few weeks passed, Darius and I made up, but he didn't like
it too much that Corey was living with us. Darius knew Corey and
of him but the fact Corey was staying with us caused Darius to
have a serious attitude. Darius would come to the house and not
speak to Corey at all. I definitely understand why he was upset

Corey was living with us but how could he be when Corey was a friend and helped us moved when Darius wasn't around. After a few months, Corey decided to leave and find somewhere else to live.

Darius and I were back together again, sometimes he would bring all the kids with him. There was always more than enough room for everyone. I treated all his children just like my very own, at one point they were calling me mom because what I did for my children I would do the same for them. Many of our downfalls in the relationship were because I always strive for better and with Darius in my life, I was praying we would be on the same page. Sometimes I would tell him some of the dreams and goals I had, and he would say, "How are you supposed to do that?" Not able to see eye to eye on a lot of things is what caused many problems in our relationship. Every time there was an argument he would take all his clothes and anything that he ever brought me, pack up and go to his mom house. How could we ever build anything if that was always his mentality and actions?

Darius was great at detailing cars. He had his regular fulltime job but would details cars on the weekend. I would always compliment him on such a great job at detailing cars. He would still talk about his own business but never initiate anything. So me being the person I am, I set up the company for him. I registered his business name online. Placed the order for the business cards online and ordered the magnets to put on the side of his vehicle. At first, he didn't have a truck for the water tanks and generator but guess what we looked for a truck, and I helped him get that. I always wanted him to be great and make moves how I was making moves, but that is where the mistake was made. Now, feeling like I was forcing him to do something he didn't want to do. Trying to make him be someone he was not. Darius ran the business for a little while, but then all of that just came to a cease. I realized if it had been him setting up the company, buying this and buying that for the business he would have appreciated it more. He was definitely content with where he was. Darius and I would bump heads a lot because of this.

CHAPTER 10

Still Working Things Out

My sister and I talked my father into coming to stay here in Orlando with us. My father was in New York for many years. He was ready for a change and agreed to come to stay. Having the extra bedroom, I offered for my father to come to stay with me. I didn't ask him for any money or anything just wanted him to get on his feet. After about 3 months a construction company hired my dad. Being from South Carolina men was taught there how to run the different types of equipment, so my dad had the skills they were looking for. It was great having my father living with me, and everyone is getting along. Both of my neighbors loved my Dad, yes, even Nick. I told my dad why I had the bad vibe with Nick and he understood. Sometimes my dad would go over to Nick house and sit down with him and his girlfriend. The girlfriend was adorable. Sometimes Nick and his girlfriend would come over if he saw my dad standing in the garage. A few months after my dad started working he met a woman named Charlene. When I met Charlene, she was ok, but I could tell she was younger then my father, nothing was wrong with that if she was willing to treat him right. A few months after meeting her my dad decided they were going to get married and he moved out. My next-door neighbor Nick and his girlfriend went to the wedding. I was amazed. About 6 months after this Nick girlfriend left him and never came back. This was when all the bitterness came, he then turned into a monster.

There was a basketball goal in my front yard for Dre and his friends to come over and shoot ball sometimes. There would be letters left in my mailbox from the HOA saying I can't have the goal in my front yard. I got so tired of the letters we just took the goal down. One day Dre and his friends were outside just bouncing the ball around and the next thing I knew my doorbell was ringing. It was the police. Nick called the cops on my kids saying the ball kept rolling in his yard and they were disturbing him. Can you imagine how upset I was that this guy would call the police on small children saying the ball is rolling in his yard? Even the police couldn't believe it, but they had to come out anyways. Things just kept getting worst after his girlfriend left him and my dad moved out.

All the back and forth with Darius we were still trying to work things out. We started going to church together and doing ok for a while. The church was like a family church. Jennifer granddad was the pastor and owner of the church. The church owned a daycare in the back, and it was the daycare Dre went to when I had him, and the same daycare Kaniya was going to. Jennifer kids went there also. Everyone knew everybody. One Sunday while at church the pastor asked Darius and me to stand up. He prophesized to us God ordained our relationship and Darius was the one for me. I held on to what the prophet said.

We were doing great for a while until one weekend we were coming back from Daytona Beach for the weekend, and we were discussing why his cell phone bill was so high, it was higher than usual. While he was driving, he asked me to call Verizon, and we placed the phone on speaker. Got Verizon on the phone and they started reviewing the bill with us. The representative said there are some charges on here from Kingston, Jamaica. So while the rep is talking, I'm questioning, Kingston, Jamaica? I told the rep there was a mistake we don't know anyone from there and definitely didn't make any calls there. The whole time Darius agreed with me. There were about three calls on there for Jamaica. He kept denying the charges. Once I hung up the phone, we discussed the calls again, and Darius was like, "I don't know anyone from there, don't know why they're on my bill."

It never crossed my mind once Darius was cheating on me. From that night I started picking up on certain things but never said anything to him about it. Now he has a job working overnight where they deliver poultry products to certain fast food restaurants. Such as Taco Bell and Wendy's. He would have to go to work from 10:00pm -7:00am. Before he left, I would always cook and make sure the food was done, so he had something to eat. One particular night before he left, Darius said, he didn't want anything to eat, he would get something later. After he left, I knew something wasn't right, but I just brushed it off. Most of the time he would call just to check in, and we would talk for a few minutes then I would go back to sleep, having to go to work the next morning. But this particular night I woke up and it was 3:00am realizing for some reason Darius didn't call. So I'm calling him, literally blowing up the phone, Darius never answers or call me back. I got up out of bed, rode to his job, circling the parking lot and my car was not there. Yes my car, because during the time something was wrong with Darius vehicle. I had a second car, so he was driving that.

At this point, I'm heated because first, this man lied to me about going to work and secondly, I know you not cheating in my car that I so gracefully let you drive until he got his back on the road. About 7:15am Darius is calling me back, after the whole night, after his shift supposedly was over, he was just calling me back. Asking him? Darius where did you go when you left the house last night? He replied, "Keya, I was at work" responding, "Darius, no you were not because I rode out to the job and the car was not there." The famous question came up, Are you cheating on me? He promised me he was not cheating.

Things were not adding up so deciding to become my own investigator I started going online to view his cell phone statements. Of course, because we were together for a while, I had all the information required to set the account up online. Pulled up the call log and saw even the next month there were some of the same charges and they're from Jamaica. Saying to myself, "I thought he didn't know anyone from this number, why are they on here for several months?" Calling, blocking out my number, no one would ever answer. Reviewing the bill, I realized there was a local number on the bill. Calls to this number would be back to back during the late night hours he worked. Pages and pages of the same number were on the bill. The calls also would be during the times he would be at work between 10:00pm-7:00am. Then the calls from that number would cease. I go back to the date Darius left the house saying he wasn't hungry, he would get something later, the same day my car was missing in the parking lot. LOL! There were no calls to that number which means he left my house and went straight to hers. At this very moment, I realized I was in the wrong line of business. Why was I not a detective or a private investigator? At this point, I knew I could be great at this.

Well, this was not the end of the investigation. I continued to view his calls online, watching that particular number. Taking the number and googled to see if I could find out any information at all. Based on Google the number came back as a Wendy's number. Thinking to myself, "The Company he worked for delivers at Wendy's, so obviously, this chick works there." I got the address based on what Google provided and sped up there, so fast I thought my car was floating. When I tell you it felt like I was on a high-speed chase, in reality, I was. When I walked into Wendy's, there is a young lady at the front counter taking orders. When she saw me, it's like she knew who I was, she looked as though she saw a deer. I didn't know if it was her or not, but she gave it away like she knew me, but I didn't know her.

There was a picture of Darius and me in my wallet. I took the picture out, just me and her standing at the counter, slammed the picture down, looked her dead in the face and said, "Do you know this guy? She said yes, that's Darius." When I looked at her in her face, her nose was spread, saying to myself, "This heifer looks like she is pregnant." Don't ask me how I knew this, it was just something I picked up on. Have you ever heard the old school saying, "If you want to know if someone is pregnant, look at the nose?" She wasn't showing or anything, it was my intuition. I asked her, "Did she know he had a family? She stated, "She knew of me."

When I realized this girl might be pregnant, my heart was crushed. So disappointed Darius could let this happen. I believed and trusted in him. Even though there were many problems, back and forth in the relationship we were still trying to make it. When I got back in the car, I cried like a baby. Before I made it home, Darius is calling me, asking why did I go to this girl job? Are you serious? I went because I asked you for the truth and you lied. You always lied until I had to take it upon myself to find out what was going on.

Asking him was she pregnant? He said yes. The only thing I could do at this point was hang up the phone. This felt like I was living a nightmare and couldn't be right. Darius goes out to cheat, not sure how long he was cheating and not only that, he get the girl pregnant. How awe full was that? Here I am trying to have a decent relationship, at the same time helping him by allowing him to use my second car to get back and forth to work, being a role model to his children, and this was the disrespectful thanks I got.

CHAPTER 11

Going Through Changes

Darius wasn't welcomed any longer, so we separated, not without getting my car back of course. No longer was I working for Bank One I decided to change my career path to work for a timeshare company. On my way to work in the mornings, which was on the way past Darius job, I would see him sitting at the bus stop. Sometimes I would blow the horn depending on how I was feeling that morning. Sometimes I would just past right by him and not blow the horn at all. I was upset and frustrated to the point I hated him. I hated that I was trying to force him to be someone he wasn't. Everyone make mistakes but damn, another baby. That cut me really deep. I didn't ever think I would forgive him, that's just how much hatred was in my heart for him. This is how it was so easy for me to ride by him in the mornings without blowing the horn because I was bitter and angry. So if he has to sit at the bus stop and wait two hours for bus 21, then so be it. At that point, I was done.

I can remember the times I tossed and turned at night, still could not believe this happened. Even though we went our separate ways, I was angry and frustrated because here I was trying to build something, feeling like I was being torn down. The world was against me and I was all alone. About a year passed, and we were finally back on speaking terms. Regardless I stilled loved him, and his family treated me well. Every time I saw Darius I thought about the other baby, it was pure torcher. Never in my life would I wish that horrible feeling on someone.

Once we got on speaking terms, Darius would always say, "Come on we can get through this, let's try and work it out." We decided to get back together and work on our relationship. I can't lie it was always in the back of my mind about the other baby and what he did. But I realized if we decided to work it out, it would not be fair to him to keep bringing up the situation. Really had to pray and ask God for forgiveness, to cleanse my heart because God was the only one that could help me at this point. Why would I agree to continue the relationship and still bring up the past? It would have been setting us up for failure again.

The relationship was back on track, but Darius was staying with his mom most of the time. He would come over during the week and stay with the kids, they were still in school and went to a different school district then mine. Many of the mornings they would have to get up really early to beat the traffic to get to school on time. Then they would come on the weekend or me, and the kids would go there. So, for the most part, it was working out.

Three months have passed since we were back together trying to work things out and I'm pregnant. Pregnant, again! Birth Control was just not my friend. After having Kaniya I had an allergic reaction to the 3-month shot called Depo-Provera, so from that point, I was running from birth control. I waited until Darius got to the house to tell him I was pregnant. With all of the back and forth I told him I wasn't going to keep the baby. No excuses, the relationship was unstable, and I didn't know what to do at this point.

I made the appointment at the clinic, Darius didn't really want to go because he didn't believe in what I was about to do and I couldn't believe it either. At that moment in our lives, we had to. Once we got there, people were outside protesting. My God, I was so embarrassed and disappointed in myself. Deep down I'm thinking of everything we have been through in this relationship, at this point I have to. This was the worst feeling ever. Everyone sitting in the clinic waiting for their name to be called after the paperwork was finished. I'm looking around, and the clinic was packed. Lord, please have mercy on my soul. I was praying and asking God for forgiveness. Feeling sick to my stomach about what I've done. When I got home, had me in tears. Lord, what have I just done? It was far too late now.

Darius and I were back and forth with the relationship again. The problems was when there was a disagreement he would pack up and leave to his mother home, there was no foundation. I couldn't depend on him to help me financially because he would always go back to where it was safe for him. A few months pass by, and here we are again. I got pregnant again. Damn Takeya, why do you keep doing this to yourself? The blame was on me, no one else's fault but mine. I knew we were having problems, so why would I continue to keep putting myself in this situation? Knowing I cared about him but couldn't depend on him to always be there. Here I am again scheduling another appointment for the abortion clinic. This time I drove myself and told them my driver was sitting outside because they will not allow the anesthesia if there is no driver. Knowing this was my second time here I was extremely embarrassed, frustrated, and depressed I allowed this to happen again.

This was against my belief and my family belief. Either my grandmother or mother had us in the church at least three times a week. Monday night was bible study. Wednesday night was a prayer meeting. Sunday's, of course, the primary day and all day, so how could I allow this to happen? My family would not have any understanding, what so ever. Everyone judges until their put into a similar situation. Before it happened to me, I said this would never in my life until I was faced with it. It still does not make it right. Knowing I was wrong, and would have to pay the consequences. It was bad enough we were fornicating then to have to go against my belief and values made me even more depressed. It's like I was in a very dark place in my life. I prayed and asked God for forgiveness because I knew I was wrong and would never allow this to happen again. This is something I've held in until this point in my life. I was too embarrassed and disgusted with myself to even mention it, even to my blood sister.

CHAPTER 12

Church Hopping

My mother decided to give her resignation to the church we all were attending since moving to Orlando, FL. She was attending the church in 1987, and when my sister and I moved in 1989, we became members as well. The church members became our family. Once I brought my first home, Dre started going to the church daycare. Then, when I had Kaniya, she attended the daycare as well. The Church was not too far from where I was living so this was perfect. Once my mother gave her letter, my sister and I decided to leave as well.

For just a little I was church hopping, well I could say just visiting different churches to hear the word but for some reason could not join. One day a friend of mine Teresa insisted that I attend this church. She advised the pastor was a mighty man of God and I would love it. I took her word and went to the church. Oh my, she was right. It was a small congregation just like in South Carolina, which is what my family was used to, being from a small town. Once I checked it out a few times Darius started coming with me. The services were powerful, but the only thing we were getting out super late. Darius loved the pastor who was great, we were attending every Sunday and ended up joining the church. I started telling my mother and sister about the services we were having, and they came. Everyone fell in love with the power and anointing that was in the service.

Eventually, my sister and mother joined the church. My mother loved the church because it was a small congregation, the prophecies and anointing were on point. When my mother joined, I was like, oh we're on to something. We formed a small praise team and would get up in front of everyone to sing and give all the praise and the glory to God. The praise team was my mother, me, my sister, and Teresa. The songs would continue until the pastor decided to get there. When we first joined we were getting out really late about 3:00pm in the afternoon on Sundays. For some reason, the pastor would get there really late, but we were so excited about the new church it didn't bother us at first.

A couple of the members were hairstylist in the church, and one of them owned a salon in a storefront. The next thing we know the church is moving and having church in the salon, which happened to be not too far from the daycare church. Even though we all left the daycare church, my kids still went there. From my understanding, there were no hard feelings we all were still like family. But anyways we followed the pastor to the salon still singing on the praise and worship team. One Sunday the pastor prophesied to Darius and read his whole life the next thing I know Darius was ready to be ordained as a deacon.

The congregation was small, so everyone knew everyone and became really close. One of the hair stylists Shira and I became really close the first time she came to my house she realized I lived next door to her cousin Harold. What a small world. They were first cousins she never realized I was the one living next door to him. All of us were standing outside one day when she came over, and Harold was looking me up and down like he wanted to say something but didn't.

One day I was walking to the mailbox and Harold wife at the time called me over and said I see you be hanging with Shira be careful with her she can be really messy and can't be trusted. I told her, "We all go to the same church together, and I haven't seen that side of her." She was like, ok but just be careful. By all of us going to the same church together we became really close. Shira would come over eat dinner or just to hang out sometimes. Also, we would travel with the pastor to different churches, just being supportive.

During this time Darius hair was really thick and long but would always keep it in cornrows. Cornrows were in style back then, and everyone had them or wanted some. Cornrows were something I never learned how to do, didn't have any patience to do them or learn. One day I called Shira and asked her if she had any available appointments, Darius wanted to get his hair braided. She booked his appointment and Darius went to get his hair braided. Two weeks later Darius decided he wanted to get his hair braided again, so I told him here is Shira information, you can call her and make the appointment if you're going to have her braiding your hair from now on.

Every two weeks Darius was going faithfully to get his hair braided. Realizing Shira would talk a lot about Harold, my next-door neighbor, which is her cousin. She would say little things like you know Harold and his wife is about to get a divorce, they're not getting along at all. Shira said, "Harold even said something about you, he said you're beautiful and wouldn't mind getting to know you. I'm like, Harold? He is married, and Darius and I are together. She would leave it alone, and we would start talking about something. One day we decided to go get seafood, and we're just sitting at the table, and Harold shows up. I said, "Shira why didn't you tell me Harold was coming?" She said," I wasn't sure if he could make it, so I didn't say anything to you about it." It was brushed under the table. Shira and I would go to gospel concerts together just trying to do positive things. Also have fundraisers for the church as well. All of us would participate. Most of the fundraisers we would have right in front of the hair salon, this is just how much we were dedicated to our church.

A few months passed, and Darius said, "I have something to tell you." I'm like, "what is it?" He said, "Shira is not your friend." "Why are you saying this Darius? What happened?" Darius started talking. He said, "Since Shira started braiding my hair she has been calling and texting me all the time, talking about you like crazy and wanting me to leave you to be with her." I was confused, wait, so you mean all this time she has been calling and texting you behind my back? I instantly started feeling sick to my stomach, feeling as though I was going to vomit. I mean this girl was at my house all the time, eating my food, smiling and laughing in my face, and being a snake behind my back? A dirty, and nasty snake. It was so hard to believe, we all were going to the same church, praising God together, worshipping God, and this slimy, so-called friend has been trying to sleep with my man behind my back. My God, what is this world coming to?

I still couldn't make any sense of this, and I asked Darius, "Why are you just telling me this now if this been going on for months? He said, "I was using her to get information about her cousin Harold, the next door neighbor." Darius said, "Shira was going back telling him Harold, and I was messing around so that she could get closer to Darius." So thinking back this is why she was bringing Harold up so much. Every time it was, Harold this and Harold that. Harold popping up at the seafood place. Shira was trying to get me to start messing around with Harold to give her even more of a reason to convince Darius I was cheating. My God, how trifling could she be? I couldn't believe it.

So mad and betrayed, I called Shira. When she answered, I asked," Shira was she trying to talk to Darius behind my back?" Her reply was, "Girl you know I would not do you like that, Darius is lying, I would not hurt you like that, were friends, I would not do that." By this time I broke down and started crying because I just couldn't understand why someone would be so evil and betray me like she did. I told Darius she denied everything he said and Shira said, "He was lying." Darius said, "Shira was blowing up his phone, and if I didn't believe him he could show me proof." I'm at home he calls me then said, he would call Shira on three-way to prove she is lying.

Darius calls Shira. She answered not knowing I was on three-way. She answers the phone calling Darius a son of a bitch. The church lady Shira, cursing like a sailor on the phone. Shira replies, "Why are you doing me like this? I love you, Keya doesn't care anything about you, and you're stupid for not wanting to be with me." Darius said, "Let me be stupid, but at least Keya knows the truth now." Not knowing I was on the other line listening. I finally said something to let her know I was there. I said, "Yes now I know the truth and Shira hung up." It took her about two weeks to call me and apologize. Shira said, "I'm so sorry for hurting you, and I'm hoping we can still be friends." I told her, "no thank you, I can't trust you, our friendship is over." From my understanding, she still came to Harold house sometimes but had no other reason to contact me, at all even though I was right next door to him. Darius advised sometimes he would be outside washing the car or doing something and she would pull up at Harold house making smart comments. I saw her one time, she was coming out of the grocery store, and I was walking in. I walked right by her like I never knew her and that was the end of her pitiful shenanigans. One day Harold was outside, and I asked him if he knew what was going on? He said yes but didn't want to get in the middle of it, because it was his cousin. I told him, "I definitely should have listened to his wife when she told me to be careful with Shira, that she was messy." But no, me being the person I am, wasn't thinking she was capable of anything like that. Maybe because we all went to church together and built a bond.

When I say, this situation made me sick. I mean literally, I was depressed and could not get out the bed to even go to church anymore. My friend Teresa also told me the pastor called Shira out one day in church and said to her, "There was a relationship she was trying to start that wasn't right. But Teresa said, "Nobody knew at the time it was the relationship she was trying to start with Darius behind my back.

It was about a year later before I could go back to this church. It wasn't the pastor fault this happened I just didn't want to see Shira ever again. By the time I decided to go back the church location changed again. I started back going, but I realized the pastor would show up later and later. We would be there for hours and hours waiting for him to show up that is why we were getting out so late, 4:00pm sometimes 5:00pm. The praise team got down to just my mother and one other lady. There were only so many songs to sing before you would be expecting the pastor to get up and preach his sermon. One day I really needed a word from God, when I got there, the pastor wasn't there yet. The praise team was up singing, three hours past and the pastor still wasn't there, yet. I told my mom... I'm gone! That was the last time I attended this church. Finally realizing there was no order. How do you expect the members to have order if the pastor doesn't? It starts with the head of the church. That day I made up my mind this was no longer the place for me. The crazy thing about it he lost some great members because of no order in the church. My mother and sister never went back either. Everyone was fed up.

CHAPTER 13

I'm Six Weeks Pregnant

I'm pregnant and excited even though many were wondering why in the hell would I get pregnant again by Darius. None of them knew about the previous situations and asking for God forgiveness. Dre and Kaniya had enough space in age between them, and now that I'm pregnant again my last two would be close in age. The crazy thing is this time in Darius family there were three of us pregnant at the same time. With this pregnancy, I gained a lot of weight. On top of that I started swelling early in the pregnancy and had high blood pressure issues. Because of this, I was going to see my OBGYN and a Specialist as well. Even though my body was tired, I still got up and went to work every day. Of course, there was no choice my bills still had to get paid.

After about my fourth month the swelling was scary, my legs were like monsters. The doctor kept telling me to elevate my feet at night and stay off them as much as possible. The job I had required only sitting and running my mouth, so I was okay when she told me to stay off my feet. The doctor also told me to stay away from a lot of salt, which I understood that could cause swelling as well.

Once I found out I was having another girl we were excited, the planning for her arrival began instantly. Everyone wanted to know what her name would be. The name came to be relatively easy, thinking about the word Trinity, 'The Father, The Son, and The Holy Spirit,' which means, 'One God' and she was the third one. Everyone loved the name and the reason behind her name.

By the time I was 8 months pregnant, I gained over 40 pounds. I was huge. At the point I was so ready for Trinity to come, this due date couldn't come fast enough. I ended up having a C- Section. Trinity came first on June 16, 2008, out of the three of us that was pregnant. Another was born at the end of June 2008, and the last was born in August 2008. The pregnancies were so close together.

My baby and I came home. Her brother Dre and sister Kaniya was there every second. Four weeks have passed Darius, and I planned the night before it's time to take the baby to go see his family. Those four weeks Trinity and I were in the house unless we had a doctor appointment to go to. I didn't believe in coming out of the house in the air too early after having any of my children unless we were going to a doctor appointment. So Darius and I were sitting on the couch in the living room one night, I advised him I feel like I'm having shortness of breath. I was breathing, but it seems as though it was taking just a little more energy than usual. Also, there was a slight pain on the left side of my upper body. Kind of brushed it off and sat on the couch until I fell asleep.

The next day we all got dressed and went down to where his family lived so they all could see the baby. Before we got there, I asked him to stop to Popeye's to get us something to eat because no one ate anything yet. I will never forget, sitting in his Aunt living room eating, this pain on the left side became unbearable, with the shortness of breath. Thinking it was gas I told Darius, "Let me step outside for a second, I'm not feeling well, let me see if I can walk this off." I was walking to the vehicle, and by the time I got to the door, the pain was unbelievable. I had no idea what was happening. It was so unbearable I couldn't walk back inside to get Darius. I couldn't move I just started crying, couldn't even yell for help. Thankfully he came to the door of the home and said, "Are you ok?" I said, "No we have to go, I'm not sure what's happening to me, I'm having shortness of breath, and this pain is making me feel like I'm having a heart attack."

Darius grabs the kids, by this time I'm lying in the back seat of the truck crying. On our way back to Orlando I told Darius, "Take me home, crying hysterically, I just want to go lay down." As soon as I told him to take me home, my phone rings, it's my mother calling from out of town because she was on vacation, with my grandmother. Lying down in the back seat of the truck, I could barely answer the phone from crying so much. My mother said, "Keya what's wrong?" I said, "Mom I'm having severe pain on the left side of my body, I have no idea what is happening to me. I told Darius to take me home, I just want to lay down." Mom said, "Keya don't you take your butt home, go to the emergency room and go now." She said, "If it's the left side of your body that's your heart and you need to get there fast." So I told Darius, "Mom said take me to the emergency room."

He rerouted, and we headed to the emergency room. When I got there, the nurse asked a few questions still crying hysterically. When I said, "Pain in my left side, shortness of breath, and just had a baby." That was it, I was rushed to the back immediately, still not understanding what was happening to me, scared as I don't know what. Darius had to wait in the waiting room with all the children. I'm sitting in the back of the room, the nurse left out and said she would be right back. In the room by myself, I began gasping for air, I couldn't breathe, and I couldn't walk! OMG! I can't breathe and couldn't get up to make it to the door to yell for help. My God, I'm about to die!! Someone else walked by and saw me gasping for air, immediately grabbed the oxygen mask, placed on my face and yelled for help.

They hooked me up to all these different machines, monitoring my heart, of course, blood pressure, and the oxygen machine I still had as well. Once I got the oxygen mask I was able to take long breaths trying to get my breathing back on track. After they ran all these tests, the doctor came in the room and advised me I was suffering from Pulmonary Embolism. Pulmonary Embolism is a sudden blockage in the lung artery. The cause is usually a blood clot formed in the legs, also known as deep vein thrombosis, but they develop in the legs and travel to the lungs. It causes chest pain and shortness of breath. So mainly the clots I had traveled from my leg and broke off into both of my lungs. This is why I was in so much pain and having a shortness of breath. She explained if I would have gone home and laid down like I started to until my mother called I would have died in my sleep.

Oh, the tears kept coming and rolling down my face I couldn't stop crying, literally a few hours ago I could have been dead. It was no one but the grace of God that had my mother call me at that very moment to tell me to get to the emergency room. What if she didn't call and I went home to sleep? All these what-if scenarios began to play back in my head. God has just spared my life.

The nurse told me it would be a while before I could go home. The whole time I'm thinking about my children. I just had a baby, and I can't take care of my little one, I was so worried. I knew she would be in good hands, but this was not something I was expecting would cause me to be away from my newborn baby.

Then eventually the nurse went and told Darius what was going on, and I would be in the hospital for a while. He had to end up taking the kids home, once my mother and grandmother got to my house to watch the kids Darius had to pack some clothes to bring for me. Thankfully my grandmother was here in Florida, and she could help watch the kids while everyone else was working. There were shots I had to get in my stomach in the morning and at night. I had to keep the oxygen mask on 24 hours a day, as well as take a blood thinner called Coumadin. For a few days, I was not able to get up and go to the bathroom on my own. The oxygen tank had to go everywhere I went.

After two weeks I was sent home. The requirements were for a nurse to come to my home and continue giving me shots in my stomach until eventually, I had to do it myself. The oxygen tank had to go home with me as well. After a couple months, the nurse stopped coming, and I was able to do the shots in my stomach myself or Darius would help. For a whole year I was required to go see a Hemoglobin doctor to prick my finger and check the thickness of my blood, make sure the blood thinner was working or if the dosage needed to be adjusted, etc. During this year my whole diet had to change. I wasn't allowed to eat a lot of green leafy vegetables. Green leafy vegetables have vitamin K, and it could lessen the effectiveness of the blood thinner I was taking, Coumadin.

Can you imagine having to go through this at the age of 29 years old? Due to the circumstances, I had to take a leave of absence from my job. Mentally this affected me as well where I went to go see a psychiatrist for the year I was off from my job. I could have been taken away from my kids at the age of 29. This situation caused a lot of anxiety and stress. Not only from the situation I went through, there started to be stress again in my relationship with Darius. The income coming in was solely based on me. I had to file for bankruptcy because there were no other options. The stress came from not being able to provide for my kids and not only that during this critical time of my life I couldn't depend on him to pay the bills.

This could have killed me. I contacted an attorney to research the rights I had to sue my doctor. The only reason this was considered is because I complained all the time to my doctor about the swelling in my legs and not once did she refer me to get any type of scanning on my legs. She just basically told me to elevate my feet at home. Per the attorney, I reached out to he advised due to the protection of the doctors the only way there could have potentially been a lawsuit if I had died from this condition, then my family could have sued. How sad was this? I could have lost my life over negligence of the doctor.

So much stress it was unreal. During this time of recovering Darius and I got into an argument where he pushed me on the bed and told my grandmother in front of her I was nothing. My grandmother said, "You mean to tell me this girl almost lost her life after having your baby, and you're sitting here telling me she is nothing." She said, "Why are you with her if she is nothing?" These were the things I was dealing with during this time of almost losing my life. How inconsiderate could you be when I needed you most? After that argument, he ended up leaving the house, and we didn't talk for a few months.

Here I was with the second child from him, risking my life but underappreciated greatly. Most of the time I had to handle things on my own because he would always leave when things got rough, and I'm left carrying the weight. From this point really our relationship went downhill. We were still trying to work things out, for me, it was really for the sake of the children.

CHAPTER 14

What Is This God Is Showing Me In My Dreams Again

Darius and I were barely hanging on by a little thread. It was so much back and forth. We were more off then on at this point. I started having dreams of Darius and my friend Teresa sleeping together behind my back. I found it kind of weird that I would be having dreams like this. She would come to my house from time to time, would see Darius helping out doing different things around the house but nothing was ever thought of her and Darius. She would say her hey and bye when she got there and was leaving.

So the first dream I had about them sleeping together I told Teresa about it. She said, "Girl, I would never do anything like that." I'm like, Oh Boy!! Haven't I heard that before? Teresa called me the next day and said, "Girl, I told my mother about the dream you had, and she said it could be someone else, which God is trying to give you a warning about." We left it alone, and I told Darius about the dream as well. He was like, "I don't even see her like that, so I'm not sure why you're dreaming about that?" I left it alone feeling uncomfortable in my spirit.

One day Teresa came to the house, and she was so excited, she said, "Girl I met this dude and he look just like Darius, he is fine."

So I'm looking at her like why are you so happy he looks like Darius? I mean she was jumping up and down, the whole nine. It was brushed off, and we went on about our business.

God kept bringing this dream to me again and usually when this happens either it is something happening at the moment, or eventually the dream will come to past. So I kept bringing this up to Darius wondering why I'm having these crazy dreams. Darius would have this smirk on his face like something was really funny, trying to make me think I was going insane or something. Teresa and I were going to school together and taking some college courses. We were taking the same class together, and I would just be thinking about what if this God is showing me is true?

So one day we got out of class and Darius was outside of the school waiting on me. Teresa walked up and said hey to Darius, he had a smile on his face trying to make me feel insecure. Or maybe I was feeling that way because of the dreams, I don't know. For some reason, he thought it was the funniest thing ever I was feeling this way. I had this dream about four times, but to Darius, I was exaggerating. Eventually, Teresa and I fell out about her going back to other people talking about me and our friendship ended.

Dealing with our relationship was getting extremely tiring, frustrating, and aggravating. Eight years have passed, and I feel definitely our relationship was coming to an end. Because I had two amazing children by this man I tried my hardest to make it work, but eventually he started playing against me. Ultimately, the disrespect would come from other women to let me know he was cheating. I held on to the prophecy given to me that God ordained Darius and our relationship. This is what kept me hanging on for so long as well as having two kids by him, I really wanted to make it work.

Eight years passed and I'm telling God, I'm tired. I wanted to know if the prophecy given to me was right, that this relationship with Darius and I was ordained by God. This is why I been hanging on so long. I ended up going back to the daycare church one Sunday. When I picked up the children one day, because now Trinity is also going, I advised I needed to talk to the pastor about something significant. For some reason, we kept missing each other, and I never had a chance to speak to him. One day the kids and I went to church, and the pastor stood up and said, "Keya I know we have been missing each other to talk, but I already know what you want to talk to me about. My heart dropped. He said, "God said, "Make the right decision for you and your children." From that confirmation, I knew it was time to let this relationship go. I held on to this for so long, but with the disrespect, it was time to let go.

One night Darius came to the house, I'm in there painting, and he was supposed to be helping me. We were decorating the living room, and all of a sudden out of nowhere Darius starts an argument. He was acting like he just didn't want to be there. After Darius said what he said, I opened the front door and asked him to leave. I never felt so humiliated in my life. Once he stepped out, I slammed the door behind him, and from that point, our relationship was over. I beat myself up how an 8-year relationship back and forth should have really been a 4 or 5-year relationship. It was a lot of wasted time and a lot of disrespect. But the great part about it was the birth of my children Kaniya and Trinity from him.

Once Darius and I went our separate ways about a year, or so later he texted me and apologized for not being able to love me how he should. For not loving me how he knew I deserve to be loved. I told him, "It was ok, there were no hard feelings, and I wasn't holding anything in my heart against him. Yes, we had issues, we had significant issues, but nothing could change at this point. The damage was already done, and the only thing left to do was continue to move forward.

Finally, the long dreadful relationship is over. One day I'm in the kitchen cooking and my phone rings. Teresa name pops up on my phone, which I haven't talked to in quite a while. She said, "Keya, your baby dad, Darius just text me." I said, "He just texted you? How did he get your phone number?" She said, "I don't know." Come to find out, when I was in the hospital about to lose my life after having Trinity this man went through all my belongings at the house and took all the SIM cards out of the old phones I had in my dresser drawers. Back then there was a SIM card. What he was looking for I guess he found. After all the questioning, asking him if he knew why I was having those dreams about him and Teresa. Making me feel insecure about the situation. The evil smirk on his face. When she called and told me he texted her, I called him and asked why? He said, "I just texted her to see how she was doing." I said, "You're an evil Son of a Bitch."

It was a couple years later my cousin Jennifer eventually said to me, "You know what you were saying about Teresa and Darius, it is true, she eventually started sleeping with him." At that point, I couldn't get upset or mad. I just knew when it was confirmed, I knew all along Darius intentions for me were evil and I'm glad I got him out of my life. He wanted to do anything he could to hurt me, and it showed. God showed me in my dreams eventually this would come to past. I wasn't going crazy. He was preparing me before it happened. Until this day, I never confronted Teresa about it, but I confronted Darius. Of course, he denied the fact it ever happened, but deep down I knew it was true. He did whatever he could to hurt me and stoop as low as possible to sleep with what used to be a close friend of mine. It made me realized how he lost respect for me a long time before we separated so why should I have been surprised? At that point I didn't feel the need to confront Teresa, it was a waste of my time. I did what any of us should do and left it in God's hands.

Eventually, Darius got to the point where he never wanted to spend time with his children. He stopped calling them and coming to pick them up. It would be 6 months at a time where my children would not see their father or hear from him, he became bitter. He really couldn't be upset with no one but himself. My children had nothing to do with the reason we were no longer together.

CHAPTER 15

My Neighbor is a Psychopath

My neighbor Nick has never been the same since his girlfriend left. He even stopped speaking to my dad, when my dad came over to visit. At one point he and my father were buddies. My dad was the only reason I tolerated Nick. Not only was he calling the police on my children from time to time. He was accusing them of throwing trash in his yard and all kinds of things. Most of the time he would be in his home, and we rarely saw him. This guy had cameras all around his home and in the trees of his yard. Everyone that came to my house would ask me, "What is up with your neighbor? Why does he have all those cameras around his home?" You would think the way he had everything set up, we were living in a million dollar home or something. He and I just didn't see eye to eye, so I started ignoring him and told my kids to stay far away from him as possible.

Since the day he rung my doorbell flicking his cigarette buds, I just picked up a bad vibe from him. I started realizing every time someone came to visit me and pulled in my driveway he would lift up his garage door and stand in the middle of the garage just looking towards us, but wouldn't say anything. This began getting creepy, as creepy as he looked.

So the saga continues when my company came over to visit his garage door would lift up. Sometimes he would stand in the middle of the driveway talking on the cell phone looking in our direction smoking a cigarette just as creepy as he wants to be. I continued to ignore him because I knew if I opened my mouth some of the wrong things would come out and would say some hurtful, evil things, so I left it alone.

One day I was leaving to go to the doctor, and there was some trash left on the side of the road that the trash truck left behind. I was running late and said I would pick it up when I got back. Returning home from the doctor the little bit of trash left on the side of the road was picked up and thrown in the middle of my driveway. I immediately thought to myself, this guy made it his best to pick up the trash and throw it in my driveway, how rude of him. So when I saw him outside I asked him nicely, "Nick did you throw this trash back in my yard?" He said, "It was yours right?" I said, "You didn't give me a chance to pick it up and what gives you the right to throw stuff in my driveway?" He said, "Your trash is your trash and walked in the house."

Trying to ignore him just didn't work anymore. The things he did were just crazy and weird. I'm in the house watching TV. My son Dre, my brother Jaquante, and Harold son Jermaine was outside playing basketball. But they were across the street at my other neighbor house because they had a goal set up beside the road. The next thing I knew all them came running inside saying, "Mr. Nick just came outside taking pictures of us." I said yelling, "What do you mean taking pictures? That's it, I'm tired of this evil bastard." My bother Jaquante was already like 6'5. So we all went over to his house. His door was opened, but there was a screened area then another screen door before you enter the home. I rang the doorbell he didn't come. I could see him sitting in the recliner watching TV. He didn't come so I started hitting the door as hard as I could for him to bring his… you know what outside. I kept knocking, knocking, and knocking, yelling at the top of my lungs to bring his evil, perverted ass out. I was so fed up with him, we were going to whoop his ass that day, then call the police. But he sat in his chair and ignored us like we were not there.

From that point on if he said anything to me, I was going to be sitting in the County jail, which is just how mad and frustrated I was with him. He didn't say two words to me, and I didn't say two words to him. Imagine having to live like that where you have a neighbor from hell. I started thinking is that why the previous owners moved? But no it couldn't be because I don't think he got like that until his girlfriend left.

Harold couldn't get along with Nick either because he would always call the police on Harold saying there was heavy traffic coming to his home. What business was it of his, Nick to continue calling the police on Harold? Even though there were many parties at Harold's house, it was not Nick's business who came to his home as long as it was not disrespecting the neighborhood.

The stress just from dealing with everything I was going through or already went through sometimes was unbearable. After the whole Darius relationship, I just didn't want to deal with anyone else at that very moment. Yes, I dated some people, ran into many crazy ones that I had to leave alone, but I was just doing me. Eventually started hanging out again but not really as much as I used to. For some reason I always found myself turning to alcohol to help relieve the frustration, anxiety, heartbroken, and loneliness I was feeling. Seem like none of my relationships worked, and I was just angry and frustrated. Even though I would see other people, there was a huge void that I was missing. Alcohol relieved the pain only temporarily.

I didn't think I was an alcoholic, I guess no one ever does, but I knew it would fill the void only for a little while. There would be times driving home and couldn't remember the next morning the ride home from the night before. That was just how wasted I would be. Looking back now I knew the hand of God was on my life because I would do this on numerous occasions. It's like God was taking the wheel and driving me home himself. Talking about the Grace of God on my life, unbelievable.

One night I will never forget, driving down Pine Hills road coming from a Super Bowl party. I got to a red light wasted as I don't know what. At the red light, I put the truck in park and fell asleep. God only knows how long I was sitting at the light because I was passed out under the wheel, not even 3 miles from my home. The next thing I knew there was loud knocking on my windows. When I heard the loud knocking on my windows, all I saw was flashing lights. One police car was in the front of me, a police car behind me and one on the side of me. One police yelled, "Open the door, and Open the door now."

When I looked around and saw the officers, I started crying because I knew from that point I was going to jail. The officers made me get out of the vehicle, crying hysterically I begged and pleaded for them to let me go home. Telling them my house was only 3 miles down the road and couldn't believe I fell asleep under the wheel. Lord have mercy, I had been doing this for years and years, why now God? God said, "Enough!" I kept begging and pleading for the police to let me go home but they asked me to walk in a straight line. I was so nervous and scared I didn't think I was drunk anymore. I heard him say someone called the police because traffic was flowing and my truck never moved. They said you were passed out under the wheel.

Just the thought of me knowing I was passed out under the wheel in the heart of Pine Hills aka Crime Hills, anything could have happened. Pine Hills has the highest crime rate in the Central Florida area, and here I was passed out under the wheel in my truck, I had at the time with 24' inch chrome rims. Somebody could have taken me and the truck. How dumb and stupid could I be not to care for my life as much as God saved my life on numerous occasions?

They put me in the back of the police car, I cried and cried until my eyes were swollen almost shut. The whole ride to the County I begged them to let me go. The officer said, "No you could have killed someone or yourself." Once I got to the County, the correction officers looked at me like they knew I didn't belong there. I was crying so bad I think they felt sorry for me. One of the correction officers kept checking on me from time to time to make sure I was ok. I had to stay the night in there until I sobered up and my sister bailed me out the next morning.

This was a wake-up call for me. Years and years from my days of going to club 436 and Hero's nightclub I rode like this, just never got caught. Many of the nights not remembering how I got home. But God said, "Enough." I was comfortable doing this because it was carried on for so long. When I was with Darius I didn't drink, alcohol was not an issue in our relationship.

I knew if I didn't get it together my life was headed for destruction. All I knew is something was missing in my life, there was that void that remains, and the alcohol cured the void but only for a period of time.

Before this even happened, I was victim to predatory lending when I purchased my second home in 2006. In 2008 the market crashed, and my house was upside down about $100,000.00 more than what it was worth. I modified my loan to try and save it, but my attorney hired advised I would never really own my home and that it would be best to let it go and start over. I did everything I could to save it, but in the back of my mind, I was ready for change and ready to get away from psycho Nick. All around I had enough, and it was time for me to start over.

Deciding to give up my home to start over I moved out. I relocated to a townhome and started renting. This was hard for me because I've been a homeowner for 15 years. But I made up in my mind if this is what it will take to start my life over this is what I will have to do. Without any help, I thought I did pretty well up to this point raising my kids alone and providing. Success comes with failure. Sometimes people fail in life and have to start over again.

I moved to another area, and the zoned schools were much better for my children. After I moved and got settled into my new place about four months later, I received a message on Facebook from my old neighbor Harold. He asked me if I heard the news. I said, "What News?" He said, "Nick, the psychopath, ex-neighbor shot himself in the head, right in the backyard where he lived." Harold said, "Before he shot himself he called 911 so they would know where to find him." When I got this news I didn't know what to do, I just couldn't believe it. Saying to myself, "God is this why it was time for me to move?"

Many things came to mind when I found out he killed himself. What if I didn't leave my home and was still there? God knew it was time for me to go. The only thing I could think was what if I didn't move, he could have tried killing all of us during this time. Because again, Nick and I could never get along. This showed me you never know what state of mind people are in and what they are going through. I kept telling my friends and family that came over to visit before I moved, something just was not right with him. What could be so horrible that would make him want to kill himself? If I didn't move beforehand, I would have been packing and moving right after that happened. I would not be able to imagine every day pulling up in my yard, knowing this man just killed himself next door. His spirit may have tried to haunt me, I don't know I'm just thinking out loud.

A friend of mine was a realtor, and he called me one day asking, "Keya, do you know you're neighbor Nick moved, I'm over here showing his property to someone?" I said no, "He shot himself in the head in the backyard." Like everyone else, he could not believe it. Even though we didn't get along, I would not have wished that on him. He was disturbed and not at peace with himself after his girlfriend left. After I left, he had no one to torture any longer. Very scary, but real.

CHAPTER 16

Meeting My Prince Charming

O h my goodness where have you been all my life? You are just what I have been praying and asking God for. Derrick was so kind and generous I just knew he was sent from God. We had the type of connection I never felt with anyone before. It was an indescribable connection. He was the kind of guy that was extremely attractive, opening car doors, buying a lot of gifts and had a remarkable sense of humor. Derrick made me feel it was all about my children and me. He was retired military for 20 years. From what I saw he had everything together, lived in a beautiful big home and drove a very nice car. God, thank you for answering my prayers and for sending me a great man. Derrick was so charming on our first date I felt an instant connection with him. The both of us came from the same background, from small towns, raised in the country. I was from South Carolina, and he was from Mississippi. I always prayed for God to send me someone that had the same background as me, so this connection was even better. I fell in love with him, my kids loved him, and my family loved him also. When we would walk in a room, he always would do something to draw attention to himself by making people laugh.

The only downfall, we lived 2 hours away from each other. He socialized with everyone and made himself fit right in, always the jokester of the gathering. Expensive gifts were popping up from everywhere, he would even open the car door for me to get in. Not saying, men, don't open car doors, but it was definitely a plus in my eyes. Such a gentlemen Derrick was, I was falling in love, and I barely knew this man.

Derrick came into the relationship as the victim, I felt so sorry for him because he advised me he was married twice, his first wife cheated on him and the second wife had another man living in the home while he was so gracefully working out of the country to make a decent living for his family. I was so hurt by his story. Thinking, how could someone do such horrible things to a great human being like himself? He made it seem as though all he did was work extremely hard and took care of his family, but kept getting cheated on. I definitely could relate to, the getting cheated on. I said to him, "You don't deserve any of this treatment at all, you're too good of a person for that, especially the ex-wife didn't have to work. Wow, she had it made, why would she do such horrible things to you? Almost every conversation was about bashing her, everything was all her fault, and that's all he talked about. I never met the women, but from his conversations, she could never do anything right and was such an awful mother. I could never figure out why he stayed in the relationship so long if she was that awe full and that's all he talked about.

Even though he was always talking about her and how much of a victim he was, I realized that his ex would call him for everything, like she didn't have a mind of her own. Or was it just me realizing that this woman, his ex, the one that had another man living in his house, had him on a puppet string. It's tough to explain, but this connection was weird. It's like he knew all of her business and she knew his, but this is his ex the one he constantly bashed. I understood they had kids together, but when you're still jumping every time she says jump, something is wrong. Anything she needed he was right there, still paying her bills, car note, but oh, of course, I was told it was for the sake of the children. It seems as even though they were not together anymore, he was still her man because he was always taking care of everything. Which I understand for the sake of the children you still have to contribute. He was taking care of everything, plus paying child support. If she wanted the kids to have $300.00 or $400.00 items, the latest phones, and gear that came out, if he didn't buy it she would turn the kids against him and tell them not to deal with their father until he purchased the items. His relationship with the children seems as though to show love, there had to be money spent. The children I haven't met yet. The children clothes and shoes had to be of a specific brand. They had to have the most expensive of everything. It wasn't the kids' fault it was the parent's fault. I would say little things to him because the situation was weird but at the same time didn't want to overstep my boundaries either. At this point, I still haven't met the children yet, not even sure if they also know I exist.

Its 4 months in the relationship, now I'm curious why I haven't been able to meet his kids yet? Whenever I'm in a relationship, I've been a part of their children's lives as well. That is just the person I am. Derrick would always respond I want to make sure we will stay together first before you meet my kids. So he says his kids have never seen him with another woman besides their mother. Ok fine, I really like this guy so, ok whatever you say. This man already met my children, he never said anything to me about not bringing the kids into the relationship. In my eyes he was already building that relationship with them so why was it a problem for me to meet his.

I'm talking to one of my coworkers one day at work, we talk like that just a few of us where we may tell what is going on in our personal life. I made a promise to them, if I haven't met his kids in six months I'm ending the relationship. Every time I would bring the topic up he would get very defensive. My mind is wondering is he hiding something from me or could this just be the way this guy does things. Six months have past and no kids, but I realized to get me away from the subject of the children he insisted on taking me to meet family in Atlanta for one of his Aunt's birthday party. I guess to get my mind off of the children. We took the Atlanta trip and met some of his family. I met his Maternal Aunts, and some of his cousins. Derrick mom could not make the trip. I was disappointed because I wanted to meet her as well. But anyway, the trip was fun. I had met a few of the family members, they were nice and welcoming to me.

As time passed, I met Derrick two sisters, mother, and father. They were nice Southern people. I realized Derrick and his mother Michelle was really close so he insisted I start calling her sometimes just to get acquainted and we did. We would talk on the phone every so often, and I would voice my concerns about how Derrick has not allowed me to meet the children. Michelle said, "girl don't let that bother you, he just want to make sure you guys work out before he brings the children around, trust me it's nothing." Michelle knew everything about our relationship because Derrick told her everything. In the beginning, I thought it was adorable, by me trying to get to know her and she was his mother. I didn't really think anything of it, maybe because our relationship was relatively new.

Months later, we got into a serious argument about him pulled on a puppet string by his ex-wife because it was always something with her, he would bend over backward, it's like if she said jump, he would be like how high. I felt like I was on the back burner, my kids and I came last to everything. Sometimes he would take his kids bowling, to the movies, or skating and would not invite my kids and I. All of a sudden Derrick need space. I gave him the space he needed, thinking that he needed time to decide what he wanted to do about me meeting the children. During this time of about two months, I didn't call him, and he didn't call me either. A couple months later he calls saying how he missed me so much and started coming around again. This relationship should have been over at this point but me still craving for the attention I so desperately needed.

It's a few days before Valentine's Day, I asked, "Babe what are we doing for Valentine's Day?" "Realizing he didn't say anything about it." Derrick replied, "Ooh, Ooh I'm taking my two girls to the Father-Daughter dance, I'm like, on Valentine's Day? The dances are usually a few days before. Derrick says, "No this one is on Valentine's Day, so of course I'm distraught. I had to get off the phone with him at that very moment. Starting to question myself, "Why am I still doing this? My whole insides were crushed." At this point, I am so ready to walk away from this crazy mess. The next thing I know, his mom is calling me, asking why I am upset about this. I told her I didn't feel as though it was fair. It's almost a year since we been together, I haven't met his kids, and now we can't even do anything for Valentine's Day? His mother

Michelle said, "Well I don't think you should be upset about that, Derrick really doesn't mean any harm." I'm thinking to myself, "This is a disgrace and an embarrassment, I can't do this anymore." It just seems like everything had to work on his terms when it was convenient for him. Almost a year had passed and still no children. I felt so stupid, and it was time to get out of this no matter how I felt about him. Feeling like something just wasn't right and my instinct was telling me something wasn't right. Feeling like God was telling me to walk away.

So the day of Valentine's he called about 5:00pm, I didn't answer, he kept calling, I wouldn't answer, I had in my mind I was done! Completely finished even though I was heartbroken and my kids were attached to him. The next day, the same calling and calling, I would not answer. A few days later he's calling again I decided to answer. Derrick asking for another chance, not to give up on him, he really cares for the kids and me. With this soft heart, I fell for it. Feeling deep down, I'm going to be alone, and I'm tired of being alone, maybe we should work this out. Every time there was a disagreement, when he came, he would bring gifts. Thinking about all the lovely gifts, I was getting, smh! I decided to still stick it out because I have a love for this guy that I've never felt before. But guess what? Two weeks later he brought the kids with him out of the blue, this is almost a year later. Because it got to the point, I stopped asking him about it, and he said anyone else would have given up on the relationship by now. In the back of my mind, I think why bring the kids now after all this time? But I kept quiet, real quiet. Finally, I get to meet the kids, 4 of the 5 came with him. Three were biologically his and his stepdaughter which he raised since she was 3, now 20. We all went out that night and had a blast together. The ice finally was broken with the kids. It got to the point the children wanted to come every weekend to Orlando, we had a bond just that tight. I think we spent more time with them than their mother because she was always in the streets running behind this one and that one, let Derrick tell it. If that's the case why are you on a puppet string? (LOL). With him and the 4 kids plus me and my 2 girls, plus sometimes my son would come over, I was cooking breakfast and dinner for 9 people, yes breakfast and dinner to save money from eating out. The kids loved my cooking. My girls and all his kids got along so well together like they were blood sisters and brothers. Every time they came we would have a blast together, it was like we all were family.

A few months after meeting the children we all took a trip to Mississippi to attend Derrick family reunion. This was a special trip because we had time to really bond with each other. All the children got along just fine there and back, which was great. Some of the family I personally already met because of the Atlanta trip and they all were there. Previously I had already met his Mother, Father, and two sisters, but for the first time met his brother at the reunion and the rest of the Mississippi family. That trip for all of us was enjoyable and exciting. All of the family was very welcoming to the children and me.

Still realizing Derrick was going above and beyond for the ex-wife. He replied, "If I don't do certain things she would get mad at me and try to turn the kids against me." I replied, "How long are you going to continue to let her control you this way?" The situation was a bizarre situation enough that I should have walked away. The connection I felt with him was different than any other I had in the past, so I decided to go with the flow.

Derrick mentioned to me one day his ex-wife began dating a woman. It was around the same time he brought the children to finally meet me. I could tell he had a problem with it because he didn't agree with the lifestyle and bringing it around his children. My God! This is all he talked about. He focused on her and her relationship. It's like his life was consumed with her issues because that's all he talked about, what she was doing. Things in my spirit started to become not at ease anymore, thinking is this the reason all of a sudden he started bringing the children around because his ex-wife finally moved on? Even though I was not at ease just little things I began to pick up on, I still overlooked. I could be wrong, but all of a sudden when she moved on it was ok for him to bring the children around after asking for a whole year. Eventually, I asked him was this the case, and he said no. It was the end of the conversation, and I left it alone.

I noticed when Derrick would come to the house he would never have his phone around and if it were around the phone would always be turned upside down, or he would always say the phone is dead. Sometimes I would question him about the phone, and he would still have an excuse. Replying to myself, "I dealt with silly stuff like this back in the day and back then it was just what I thought it was." Hell, years ago I did it myself when I was up to no good so why would it be any different when Derrick is doing the same things? You would figure he is almost 50 years old and you're still doing childish stuff I was doing when I was 21 years of age? Something is not right. If there was a disagreement, he was always picking up the phone, calling his mother.

In the beginning, I thought him always calling his mother was really funny and cute while I was still getting to know her as well. But after a while I realized every time there was a disagreement he would not answer the phone for me but would pick up the phone and call his mother, telling everything happening in our relationship. On numerous occasions, Derrick would just ignore my calls but would talk to his mother, and she would be calling me, asking why this and why that? Sometimes I wouldn't hear from him for a few days later when he was in the wrong never apologizing for anything. Every situation was turned around on me to make it seem as though I was always wrong for questioning anything he did.

One day Derrick decides he wanted to take his sons to the football game to watch their favorite team. So I said, "Ok no problem, you boys have fun, go enjoy yourselves." I'm messing around on Facebook one day just browsing and ran across a picture of them at the game, but wait a minute! It wasn't just Derrick and his sons in the picture, it was the whole family, all the kids, the girls too, and last but not least, his ex-wife! All of them were wearing matching football jerseys. I'm looking at the picture like this SOB lied to me, and he said he was taking his sons to the game so how did the whole family get there in matching football jerseys? Everyone smiles in the picture like one big happy family while my kids and I are sitting home. Did we get an invite to the game? No, no invite what so ever.

Later that night Derrick called me like nothing was wrong, acting as usual as can be. Not knowing I saw this picture on Facebook. I just sent it to his phone waiting on a response. During the call he pulled up the text, asking how I got the picture. What do you mean? How I got the picture. All I want to know is why did you lie to me? And if we were doing family outings, why were my kids and I not invited? He lied saying, He told me they all were coming when I knew for a fact he didn't, but clearly, I wasn't supposed to know. Can you imagine how that made me feel? I and my kids sitting at home while he, his ex-wife, and all the children went to a professional football game together and we didn't get an invite. By me questioning him with this Derrick didn't apologize or anything, he just hung up the phone like I shouldn't have asked him about anything at all. A couple days later, you know who's calling? "The Mother," talking about, "they didn't ride to the game together in the same vehicle" like that was supposed to make me feel better because they rode in separate cars. Derrick went a whole week without talking to me and answering my calls. Basically, it was a slap in the face. I thought it was incredibly disrespectful, but of course, he and his mother saw different. When we did finally speak the issue at hand was swept under the rug like nothing happened. He would never bring up the topic at hand and want to discuss our problems. I had to hear it from his mother.

When we were good, we could laugh and joke around with each other, having fun together. I would always tell him when he came around how good he looked, still giving him compliments. Realizing no matter what I did he would never compliment me on anything. I wouldn't get, "Babe you look great today, Babe thank you for this or thank you for that. I was always the one making him feel like a million dollars, putting him up on a pedestal. It just seems as though everything was still about him, always soaking in the compliments, never apologizing, and all conversations reverted back to praising him. He was an attention seeker, always needed attention. Sometimes when we were around friends, his conversation would always be about him. How he did this and how he did that, it would still turn around to something about him. Always wanting the spotlight on him. Mr. Funny guy is in the room. Some of his conversations also would be jokes about me, some were embarrassing, and some were funny, but he would always make the joke centering on me.

For some reason I was so in love with this man, failing to take heed to all the warning signs. I so desperately wanted someone in my life I ignored a lot. With Derrick having a stable career background, having himself together and the instant connection we had when I first met him, I just knew he was the one for me. As previously in my relationships, I didn't have anything even close before. When I first met him, he was coming to Orlando every weekend and sometimes during the week. In the beginning, it was like he was love bombing me, so into me. After three months of being in the relationship, he told me he loved me.

Eventually, Derrick and the kids would take out the time and go pick my father up, spending time with him. This melted my heart because I never had anyone in my relationships to do this and care for my parents as he did. He presented himself as a well respectful gentleman, an older guy who had it all together. He and my dad got along great. Derrick children even started calling my dad, granddad. That is just how close they got to him. This definitely was awesome in my eyes.

Derrick definitely had some great qualities not only building that relationship with my dad but my kids as well. They loved him and grew so attached to him. He would spend time with them and get to know them, sometimes without me they would go out for ice cream, or he would take them shopping, etc. Something a real man should do when there are children involved. Derrick seems as though he really cared for my children. That drew me even closer to him. When Darius saw the way Derrick was with Kaniya and Trinity, he switched his game up toward the girls and began picking them up every other weekend. I guess it took him to see another man taking care of his kids before he stepped up to be a father. I didn't have to worry about Darius from that point forward. Derrick and I would go out and have a really great time together. He would always tell me no matter what he has my back, and he is never leaving, that he would still be here for my children and me.

I knew what Derrick was telling me, but sometimes his actions would speak differently. Deep down my spirit was not at ease, and my intuition was telling me different. Even though there was no boundaries set with the ex-wife and Derrick mother always in our business, I continued on the journey with him anyways afraid of being alone. Derrick was a secretive person. He didn't want me on any of his social media pages, and if I posted a picture of us and tagged him in it, he would remove it from his page. Some of his excuses were he didn't want anyone in his personal business or to know who he's dating. Ok, I would be okay with that but why was it OK for him to still have pictures of his ex-wife on his social media pages and he refused to take them down? Call me Petty Betty! But why was it ok? Every time I would ask him to take them down. I was called insecure and jealous. We have been in a relationship for two years now why do you still have your ex-wife pictures on your social media page when you have an issue with me on your page?

This bothered me so from time to time we would argue about it, Derrick would get upset, call his mother and tell her about it. The cycle of no communication sometimes would repeat itself. I just couldn't understand why a man would put his significant other through this if we were in a relationship? I just couldn't make sense of it at all. Why was this relationship all about him and his feelings? Mine didn't matter at all. I couldn't understand why he didn't allow me to walk away when my mind was made up previously if he was going to treat me this way. I just couldn't understand it. Slowly but surely I felt as though I was losing myself to this man.

I would feel as though I was about to fall apart. Something in the relationship just was not right, not right at all. There would be many times I would be at work feeling as though I wanted to run to the bathroom and cry. Always trying to put my best foot forward with a smile but deep down on the inside, I was very unsure about my relationship. It seems as though no matter what I did to show I loved him, it just was not good enough. There was a complete void. An uneasy feeling, just couldn't put my finger on it.

It's like being in a relationship where your intuition is telling you something is not right, but you have become addicted to this person. The little attention you are getting from him for a short period of time has you wanting more and more even though you know you should have left a while ago.

CHAPTER 17

More Lies! The Pedestal Is Breaking!

S till putting Derrick on this pedestal he tells me he has to go to Atlanta, GA to see one of his oldest sons from his first marriage. There are three sons from his first marriage, which two of them lived in Atlanta. He says, "The youngest of the three really need him right now, and he has to make this trip." My reply, "Ok Babe." I never questioned anything twice as to why he was making this trip. Why should I? At this point, he didn't give me a reason to think anything different. The whole trip there we were on the phone just laughing and talking. He was a jokester, always having something funny to say. He made the trip safe, and that was that. Didn't have anything on my mind, we said our good-byes and I would speak to him later.

Later that night he steps outside to call me just to check on me and tell me he is having a great time with his sons and grand-children. Derrick also tells me his brother from Mississippi is in Atlanta that weekend as well because his brother girlfriend lives there. So I said, "Awesome, you all are in Atlanta this weekend, everyone will get to see each other." We talked for a little while then he said he had to go and will talk to me tomorrow. The next day he called me to show some shoes from Foot Locker that I loved. I said, "If they have my size, please get me a pair." Didn't talk to him anymore that night. Every night we would talk on the phone before bed if he weren't in Orlando. I realized this night he didn't call me or anything, but I didn't worry because I knew he was bonding with his sons that he rarely gets to see, so it wasn't a problem or anything. The next morning I still have not heard from him. Derrick called late in the afternoon about 5:00pm talking about what a great time they all had, and he was back on the road. He was happy to see his sons, grandchildren, and brother.

Leaving Atlanta, he is on his way to Alabama to stay for a while, and unfortunately, his Job sent him there. We were not sure how long he would be there, maybe a few months. But the job was paying for the hotel accommodations and food of course. One night I'm just browsing Facebook, Derrick son page and he posted a picture of their weekend. When I saw the picture, my heart dropped. In the picture, it was Derrick two sons in Atlanta, his grandchildren, Derrick and Derrick first wife. I'm saying to myself, "How was the first wife in the picture? He didn't tell me she was there. She doesn't live here in Atlanta, she lives in Chicago. How did she so happen to be in Atlanta the same weekend Derrick was there? All of them were at a hibachi restaurant sitting at the table singing happy birthday to the ex-wife.

Derrick lied to me this whole time about the reason he actually went to Atlanta. He didn't go because his youngest son of the three really needed him like I said previously. He went to celebrate his first wife birthday. They all made plans that weekend to meet up in Atlanta. She flew in from Chicago, and they all met in Atlanta where the sons lived. I was so sick and disappointed the whole weekend this man was lying to me. Once again I was made out to be the fool. The one that I loved deeply and would bend over backward for was telling me he loved me but continuously lying to me like I didn't deserve to be respected.

I began questioning myself in the relationship. Why was I not good enough for him? I have shown him in every way I am here for him as well as his children, why was he treating me this way? So Derrick is in Alabama! I called to ask him why did he lie to me about the trip to Atlanta. Why was he able to tell me about everyone on the trip but failed to say to me they all planned the trip to celebrate his first wife birthday? This guy showed no remorse what so ever. He never said, "Keya, I'm sorry I lied to you." Nothing. Nothing, what so ever. You know what he told me? Derrick said, "Well Keya, she is one of my best friends, there is nothing she wouldn't do for me. If I need anything, she is there." Can you imagine how this made me feel? I have been in a relationship with you, never cheated, bending over backward for you, I'm your significant other, why am I not your best friend? You have never said anything even as close to me about the bond we have. How am I supposed to take you telling me another woman, whom you were married to for many years is your best friend? Why am I here? Why am I even in this relationship with you? It seems as though I wasn't needed for anything. Is this why our relationship appears as though it is a secret? Because you're trying to please everyone else? Not once did he offer to take me with him to meet his other sons. Almost feeling as though I was in a relationship by myself. Indeed I was because I was the one pouring and pouring myself into him. It was a one-sided relationship.

Derrick would never answer any of the questions. He turned the whole situation around on me and said I was incredibly insecure. He would never apologize for anything, Derrick went several days without talking to me. The whole situation was turned around on me. I started questioning myself. Maybe I should not have said anything to him about this, I should have just left it alone, we would be ok now, and he wouldn't be mad at me. He was using reverse psychology and manipulation to make it seem as though it was my fault. Derrick even took it as far to say he didn't know if he still wanted the relationship any longer. I would realize with him every time I tried to talk about something serious he would always change the subject by cracking a joke or just moving on to something else. When he would give me the silent treatment for a few days when he came back around we would never discuss the issue at hand. He would come back around like nothing happened.

Derrick even took it as far as telling me I have gained weight and he didn't want a fat woman. I mean is this anything you really say to a woman that you say you love. I'm the type of person that would never let myself go. If I'm gaining weight, I know when to pull back from the table if need be. I've always taken care of myself and cared about my appearance. Anyone that knows me can tell you that. It was just one excuse after another. I never said anything to him about the additional 20 lbs. he gained since we started dated. I would have never said anything rude to him about his weight. It is one thing for us to work out and support each other but not put each other down. I would never do that to him.

A couple days later Derrick mother Michelle, was calling. Derrick told her everything that happened. His mother, Michelle, said to me if she were Derrick she would not have told me either the reason for the trip. How stupid was I to continue to stay in this so-called relationship? It was one-sided either his way or no way at all. I guess I had to be really stupid with my eyes closed because I stayed in the relationship. I would always ask Derrick why is it you still call your mother every time there is a disagreement? I didn't understand why his mother when a man is 48 years old. This was something I never experienced before, with someone always calling their mother involving them in their personal relationships. Derrick excuse was because he would want to get another women point of view on this and he can always talk to his mother. We could never talk our problems out, he would call his mother with the issues then his mom would call me. I mean don't get me wrong it's ok to confide in your parents on specific topics, but when there is utterly no privacy at all in your relationship, then that's a problem.

CHAPTER 18

The Engagement

One day Jennifer stopped by, and we were in the kitchen talking. Jennifer has been around me for years and years since we moved to Orlando, so she knows me like the back of my hand. I was just telling her some of the things I was experiencing in my relationship with Derrick and just wanted to get her input or advice on some of the issues I was having. Explaining to her, I was accused of being insecure, and every time Derrick is at fault he never admits he is wrong or would never apologize. He would look me in my face and wouldn't say anything at all. Always jumping to another subject like my thoughts didn't matter. I had no idea what was going on. He would treat me like, I didn't have the right to question him about anything. That is the way he made me feel. I also told her how every time he calls and tells his mother everything. There was no privacy at all in our relationship. What grown man, damn near 50 years old does that? Tell his mother everything happening in his relationship without working it out with his significant other. It is just unheard of and unreal. I never experienced anything like this before.

Jennifer tells me, "Girl you know I have a degree in Psychology, and there is a disorder such as a Narcissist, they never admit to wrongdoing, never apologize, and always have you thinking it's your fault. It is a mental personality disorder called, Narcissistic

Personality Disorder." I said, "Whhhhhaaaattttttt, what are you talking about? I've never heard of anything like that before." "Girl I don't know about all that, I wouldn't take it that far." Jennifer said, "Girl, it's real, but you don't hear too much about it." Me, always brushing something off, I said, "never heard of it but ok and I left it alone."

A few months past and it is time for our family reunion in South Carolina. I asked Derrick was he going to be able to come? Understanding because he was in Alabama working, didn't think he could make it. On top of that he was so called still upset I questioned him about the whole trip to Atlanta. Making me feel like I was the one that lied to him about something. Derrick kept saying he didn't know, of course, wanted me to beg him to come. It was not his first time coming to South Carolina with me. He knew every time we went all of us had a blast so of course he wasn't going to miss that trip.

All of a sudden one day we were talking and Derrick was like, "yes when we go to South Carolina we will do this and that." I'm thinking to myself, "I thought you didn't want to go, just wanting me to beg him." I got to South Carolina first, and a few hours later he pulled up. We hadn't seen each other for a few months, only on face time that was it. The crazy thing is the entire time he was in Alabama he didn't ask me to drive up to meet him or anything. A few times he drove back to Atlanta to see his kids and grandchildren but never asked me to come to Atlanta, meet him, or any interest in seeing me at all .

Saturday we all got dressed for the family reunion day and headed to the location. Each family had to introduce themselves.

So my mother got up and headed towards the front of the room to introduce all of us. My mother introduced my brother Jequante first. Then my sister, Kisha and her family stood up for my mother to introduce her, her husband, and my nephew, my niece, was in Texas at the time. Once my mother got to my table she introduced myself, as her daughter, Derrick as my friend, Kaniya, Trinity, and DeAndre. My God, why did my mother introduce Derrick as my friend in front of everyone? He was highly embarrassed. He was trying to figure out why my mother was considering him to be in the friend category. Once everyone introduced their families we were asked to line up for food. When we got in the line, Derrick called himself straightening and questioning my mother about why he was still in the friend zone. He said, "I was out the friend zone a long time ago." My mother responded, "I thought when you invited your parents and sisters to my daughter Kisha house, to celebrate Christmas that was it! I thought you were throwing in the towel and proposing to my daughter Keya. Everyone thought you were." Derrick said, "Even so I'm still no longer considered her friend anymore, I'm her man." My mother said, "I call it how I see it." After that, the conversation ended really quickly. But I could tell he didn't like it at all.

The reunion is over, and everyone is heading home 95 south, even Derrick, his contract in Alabama was over. When he got back, he found out there was a sale date for his home. The home was going through foreclosure, and he had two weeks to get out. At this point, Derrick had no place to stay. He was back and forth from my home to his sister home. There was not a problem with it. The only issue was he had to travel a couple hours to his job back and forth.

Two weeks after the reunion has passed and I'm just getting home from work. Trying to figure out what we were going to eat. Derrick, Kaniya, Trinity, and I are all downstairs in the kitchen. I have my back turned, and Derrick said, "Here you go, it was a Pandora bracelet. The smile was so bright on my face, I'm always thankful. Then he pulled out a box, calling my mother on Face time, he gave me an engagement ring and asked me to marry him. I was so happy and excited it was the last thing I was expecting from him. He gave me the ring, but he also said we are not going to get married right now, let him decided when we will get married. My smile gradually went away. I was happy but why did you have to say that at the moment? You asked me to marry you? Why it is all up to you when we get married? Isn't this supposed to be mutual?

I was still happy that he gave me a ring. I told all my family, friends and coworkers. I even posted the picture on my social media. Excited but deep down something is just missing or not right. When you ask someone to marry you, both are supposed to come to a mutual agreement as to when we should plan the wedding. I just went with the flow. One day I'm talking to his mother Michelle on the phone, and we are talking about the marriage. She said to me, "Let Derrick plan everything and determine when the wedding will be, you can't take over what he has planned. He will make the decision when you'll get married." Pulling the phone away from my ear, looking at the phone like, did I just hear this correctly? Was I really hearing this from her? This is supposed to be one of the happiest moments of my life, and all I hear is the word "CONTROL" in the back of my mind. Why can't we plan this together? This marriage will change both of our lives, not just his. Furthermore, what does this have to do with his mother and how can they both treat me this way? This whole situation was stressing me out.

One day we were discussing my business I started called, "Country Girl Soul-food and Seafood LLC." We discussed Derrick being a business partner to help with the business since we were together. I thought it was a great idea. So I was trying to get this specific vehicle for the longest, a vehicle I wanted for the business, and things just didn't work out. Even though I was considering him as my business partner, I still wanted to get this vehicle on my own instead of allowing Derrick to purchase it. He called his mother and told her, "I didn't want him to go get the truck." She then called me and said, "He wants to get the truck so let him get it." Derrick wanted to purchase the truck for himself, but he stated, when I needed to use it, I could. For some reason, he insisted on asking his parents to co-sign for this vehicle just to be able to say he was the one that purchased it. It wasn't like he was getting the truck for the business only, this was going to be his everyday vehicle. His dad helped him get the truck. Once Derrick got the truck he said nothing else about helping me with the business. It was like a slap in the face with him saying, Ha! Ha! I got the truck, and you don't. But the whole idea of the truck was to help me with the business. These were the games he played. At this point I'm feeling as though it's a competition not a relationship.

Not only was I dealing with the ex-wife issue with him on a puppet string, Derrick knowing all her business and she knew his. I was dealing with Derrick telling his mother everything. There were no boundaries what so ever. Every time I would say something he would make me feel so bad for bringing it up. Don't get me wrong his mother and I had some great conversations but he did everything she told him to do. I could not figure this situation out for the life of me. I started feeling as though I didn't fit in this equation anymore or should I say, I never really did. Well, I was feeling this a long time ago but afraid to leave, not wanting to be alone and start over. Plus I loved him, at least I thought I did.

From the point, I was given the engagement ring on my finger seemed like all hell broke loose. We were arguing almost every day. Derrick would make me feel like I didn't know anything at all. He began to belittle my intelligence. Everyone was still telling me congratulations, my friends, coworkers, and family, not knowing deep down I was unhappy and feeling miserable because of all the stress from his side of the relationship. Every time I brought up the wedding or marriage he would say, "I told you not right now, let me do this."

Derrick would tell me an engagement does not guarantee marriage, it's the both of you still getting to know each other." Basically letting me know it's not promising we will get married. At this point, we have been together for three years, and you mean to tell me our engagement still means we are getting to know each other? I can't believe this was happening to me. I started feeling like a walking zombie. At work wanting to break down and cry but still not wanting to let go. I felt as though I was losing myself but still not wishing to let go because a part of me always wanted to make this work and hoping it would all change all of a sudden. Thinking of the time already spent on this relationship, not wanting to start over. Knowing I deserved better but just could not walk away even though God told me over 2 years ago.

People kept asking me, "When is the big day, and I couldn't respond because I had no idea." The way I was feeling on the inside made me really sad and hurting. Feeling like I was going to break down at any moment because this was not the way I visualized my engagement or one of the happiest moments of my life to be. Why did he give me a ring if all these stipulations came with it? Sometimes on my way home from work, I would just cry because I felt as though I was giving my all to a person that didn't think I was good enough for him. No matter how much I poured into this person life, emotionally and mentally he was taking every little piece of energy I had, but still staying in the relationship and not wanting to walk away.

CHAPTER 19

Prince Charming Turned Into A Frog

L abor Day weekend was coming up, and Derrick said he had plans to go to Mississippi, where he is from, to meet up with some of his homeboys he hasn't seen in a long time. Since he said it was just his homeboys, I figured that is why he didn't ask me to go. I told him, "Derrick I'm surprised you didn't ask me to go with you on this trip." "Derrick said, it's only a whole bunch of guys no women at all is coming." So I said, "Ok since you will be gone Labor Day Weekend, the kids, myself, and mom will go to the beach while you're gone." The conversation ended.

One day Derrick showed me a picture of him when he was in high school, we laughed and laughed. It really didn't look like him at all, that is why it was so funny. A few days later I saw that someone shared this same picture on his Facebook page and said, "Class of 89, 30th High School Class Reunion, Labor Day Weekend, can't wait to see everyone there." Hmmmm!!! My mind is thinking, 30th High School Class Reunion? Labor Day Weekend? That is the same weekend Derrick said he was going to Mississippi to hang out with his homeboys and no women where coming.

Takes a deep breath! Did this man lie to me again? And why would he not tell me the truth that it was his 30th High School

Class Reunion? Well, the only answer is, He didn't want me to go! My mind began to wonder was he meeting someone else there. Or was he taking someone else with him, why didn't he want me to go? Why would you not want to take your fiancé with you to your 30th High School class reunion? If two months ago you asked me to marry you and your going to your 30th High School Class Reunion, why would you lie to me and say no women would be there like it's just a men's retreat or something? We talked, and I questioned him as to why he told me he was going to meet up with some of his homeboys and not tell me the truth about where he really was going? Derrick replied, "I told you the truth, and I'm not going to the class reunion. I'm going for the reason I told you I was going." Still denying the fact of the truth. I was so hurt, you couldn't imagine how this made me feel, indeed rejected and heartbroken. Again feeling like I wasn't good enough for him to take me around people he went to school with and to think I was engaged to this man.

I cried, cried, and cried until there were dry tears. It's like I knew I deserved better but couldn't get out. Before Derrick left for that weekend to Mississippi, he basically abandoned my kids and I. Instead of us communicating face-to-face and getting to the bottom of his deceitfulness and lies he sent a text and ended the relationship. Yes, a text, from a grown 48-year-old. After all, the emotional and mental abuse, all I deserved was a text message to end a three-year relationship. I offered for us to go to counseling for some help but he refused. He refused because his mother was his counselor and he didn't feel as though he was wrong about anything in the relationship. I was blamed for it all. That whole Labor Day weekend videos and pictures were showing Derrick having a blast at the Class Reunion with everyone else. The one he lied about and was not going to while leaving a whole fiancé at home. This man was going to attend this event like he was already single to get the attention he always craved for, this is how he survived or lived, off the attention of others . After three long, stressful years Derrick abandoned us because of his wrongdoing. His pride would not allow him to say sorry or apologize for any of his wrongdoing. I was supposed to accept whatever he dished out and keep my mouth closed. It was a total control and manipulating issue he had. He was very deceptive and manipulating. I completely lost myself. It's like this man was living two separate lives. I just could not understand it for the life of me. No matter how I tried to turn the situation around to make sense of the relationship, I couldn't.

This whole relationship I ignored the red flags because desperately I wanted someone in my life. I was happy with the little attention I was receiving from him, and I put him on a pedestal because he came into the relationship as a victim. Playing the blame game. It was everyone fault but his.

All the problems we had in the relationship was blamed on me, not once was I unfaithful to him because I cared just that much. I just couldn't figure out how you can maliciously continue to lie and lie to someone that loved you and had your back 100%. I fell in love with his children and did for them like they were my own. When he lost everything, he worked so hard for I was there for him. No matter how much love I continued to show him the more he lied to me and layers of his mask slowly kept peeling away. His mother, Michelle called me about the whole Class Reunion trip and said I wouldn't have wanted to go anyways because they have huge mosquitos up there in the country. I said, "You're probably right but why lie like you were hiding something, why lie about it?" Of course, she noted Derrick originally was not going to the reunion but somehow ended there anyways. Yeah Right!! Of course, that was her way of taking up for him to seem as though he didn't lie to me. She also told me we didn't need to be getting married and we needed to start over as friends.

At this point, I felt like starting over as friends were just un-real to me. I have given him three years of my life, and you want us to start over as friends, no I'm not doing that. I'm tired and exhausted, I have given you all of me, and it was just not enough for you. Everyone was put before me in the relationship. I was definitely on the back burner, and no matter what I did, it just was never enough.

CHAPTER 20

Realizing I'm Broken

O nce our relationship ended, I cried and cried, asking God, how and why my relationship had come to an end. Deep down I knew why because God told me to leave two years before this happened and I didn't, so he removes Derrick instead. Feeling like I poured everything into this man and gave him all of me to the point I completely lost myself. Beginning to question me, why was I not good enough for him? At this point in my life, I was so broken, not wanting to be here any longer. I was so ready to throw in the towel. Days I called in from work not able to get out of bed because life for me was over. Staying home in the bed with no strength or energy to face anyone. I couldn't even get out of bed for the sake of my children asking God to just let me die and no longer live. Didn't want to face the pain and hurt I was feeling. I'm tired of giving, giving, and giving, pouring into people and just wasn't enough? Suicidal thoughts running in my mind, telling myself I'm no longer worthy and suitable for anyone at this point. God please just let me leave. Many times I got in my car thinking what if I just drove off the cliff of a bridge? I'm better off dead. The only thing I was thinking about was my children. Would my children have the support system they need? I just knew I no longer wanted to live God and face this detrimental pain! I no longer want to fight this battle any longer. I'm empty, and I no longer have anything to offer.

Crying out to God in my prayer closet every day. This man was supposed to be my husband. Why would you allow this to happen to me? I told everyone we were getting married. Forcing myself to be at work genuinely empty inside. Many times I would have to get up from my desk and go into the bathroom, trying to hold back the tears because I was so broken and devastated. When I was off on the weekend it got to the point there was no energy to leave the house. I even had to put a hold on running my business, "Country Girl Soul-food and Seafood LLC." There was no energy to face people. The reality is, I didn't recognize myself, completely lost, in what I thought was love. I knew at this point in my life I was not ok and didn't care what happened to me. I was completely empty inside, tired and exhausted.

Distancing myself from everyone including my family. Realizing that many knew my relationship ended but no one ever asked me, "Keya are you ok?" Just those words alone "Keya are you ok?" No one ever asked! The answer would have been, if anyone asked screaming, "No I'm not ok! I'm not ok! This man took everything I had to offer and left, I'm not ok!" Because no one ever asked, it was just God and I fighting this battle alone. Fighting this battle I wanted to end sooner than it should. People fail to realize even the strongest of the strong need to be checked on from time to time to make sure they're ok. Even the strongest fall and need encouragement just as well as anyone else to get back up again, but I didn't have any of that. At that moment in my life, I just needed someone to say, "It's going to be ok." It broke me even more because no one took out the time to ask, was I ok? Feeling all-alone and that no one cared about what I was going through.

Everyone has known of me to be an energetic individual, who has always made moves, still able to move forward no matter what happens in life. But this situation was taking my whole life because I believed in Derrick and was highly disappointed. He was put on this pedestal by coming into my life as a victim. When everything started happening each time was a disappointment because of the respect I gave him, but he let me down. Have you ever just believed in someone so much and gave your all to be let down and disappointed? I had no idea how to pick myself up after this. I just wanted it all to end.00

Crying out to God in the secret place became a routine. At this point in my life, I needed answers. Answers as to why this was happening. Blaming God and upset with God for my pain and frustration. Yes, I was definitely bothered with God despite what he told me to do. He allowed this man to walk away. Crying out to God one morning I heard a voice, the voice of God that said, "Why are you crying? Why are you crying when I have just saved your identity, I have just saved your life?" "Have I not shown you at all times who I am in your life? I have promised to never leave you or forsake thee." "My child I have always walked with thee, even when you thought you were all alone, I was there. You have prayed and asked for protection, and that is what I gave thee." Immediately stopping all the crying dead in my tracks, looking around because I knew what I heard clearly.

Questioning God, asking myself "What does God mean he has saved my identity?" Clearly, I hear his voice again saying, "Go back and do the research on Narcissism." Narcissistic Personality Disorder, the same disorder Jennifer was trying to explain to me months ago, but I brushed it off. Rushing out of my prayer closet, immediately turning on my computer, I began to do the research. When I tell you the information on this disorder blew my mind, reading, reliving everything I went through in this past relationship and his behavior. It was everything I was going through in the relationship with Derrick, he has been exposed! It brought me back to thinking about a comment is ex-wife made on social media one time that she is no longer mentally and emotionally abused. I asked Derrick about it, what did she mean by that and he said he had no idea what she was talking about. Not realizing while I was in the relationship, the same things were happening to me.

So while doing this research on Narcissistic Personality Disorder, I found out it is a mental condition in which people have a high demand of admiration. They have to feel extremely important at all times and have a deep need for excessive attention. There is a lack of empathy for others, and they never apologize for any of their wrongdoing. They're merely and genuinely unaware of their actions and the effects they have on their surroundings. They lack emotional keenness or sharpness of thought and intelligence to process the ramifications of their actions at the moment.

For some reason, these people think they are some type of God and who are you to question them about anything they do? They never feel anyone is ever good enough for them. This is why the Narcissist is always looking for something better that does not exist. The truth is these people are empty on the inside and very unhappy with themselves, to the point they feed off of their victim's energy to make them feel better. As evil as it may sound, these people love to see their victims suffer because it helps them to feel empowered and in total control of you. The Narcissist love playing mind games, have you thinking it's all about you, but really they're living a double life and sucking all the energy and life out of you. They disappear when being questioned about wrong-doing because the Narcissist feel as though their perfect people and can never be accused of doing anything wrong. In a few days, they will reappear like nothing happened and never want to discuss the issue at hand. None of the problems are ever resolved. Once the idolization period is over, which occurs at the beginning of the relationship by love bombing you, they abandon you and move on to their next prey and start the cycle all over again. Once their victim realizes the Narcissist is not who they say they are and the mask has been lifted, they will abandon you like he or she never knew you because they refuse to be exposed.

These people have an empathy level of a 4-year-old due to something traumatic that happened in their childhood years. Usually, it was lack of love or emotions received from their mother when they were a child, or possibly his mother could have worshipped him so as a child by always making her son feel like he was better than others. Because of this the son grows up still needing to feel worshipped and admired at all times. This is why Derrick always looked to the mother for answers and needing her approval on everything. Narcissist grows up into adults, even requiring that breast milk and admiration from their mothers to think highly of themselves, when really on the inside their damaged, soulless people. All they care about is themselves. Pulling whatever energy they can from other people just so they can love themselves, feel empowered by all the attention and admiration received from others. This person never loved me as a person, he just liked the way I made him feel and put him on a pedestal. The

Narcissist will have everyone around them fooled because of the false persona they present.

Crazy and weird, right? Demonic and Satanic power? Asking God, "What type of evil, demonic spirit is this? How did I get myself attached to this mess? Yes I know, deep down people with this personality disorder is scared and broken. Hurt people will definitely hurt other people. They will do whatever it takes to get that attention and admiration from others even if they have to go outside of their relationships. It's all about them, and they do what it takes to fulfill their needs only, while you're dying on the inside continually trying to please them. They're known to be excessive serial cheaters because again once the admiration from their partner is gone or that person is no longer praising them due to the layers of their mask falling off, they will do whatever it takes to find someone else that will worship them. Even if it means to abandon their current relationship. These people are always looking for better nothing ever satisfy them. They're looking for someone to continually give them the praise like their mother always did.

Once the partner of a narcissist begins to realize the narcissist isn't who he or she initially presented themselves to be, and starts to question about their wrongdoing, the Narcissist will start giving their partner the silent treatment and disappear for days until he feels the victim is ready to obey and stay under his control without having to answer any questions about their wrongdoing. This is the mind games and manipulation tactics they used to control their partners because their empathy stopped developing at an early age. They're not able to relate to some of the things you're trying to communicate to them in a relationship because everything has always revolved around them. Their unaware of the pain and suffering they are causing the victim because they're not able to relate.

Everything played back in my mind about this relationship, crying nonstop. This is why Derrick always called on his mother, and she made all the decisions for him. I felt as though he didn't have a mind of his own. He felt the need to continually tell his mother everything that was happening in our relationship for her approval and validation. I will never forget. His mother Michelle called me one day, and we were talking, and she said to me, "You know my son tells me everything right?" The only thing I could say to myself was, "Lord how did I get into this mess?" Even though I loved Derrick, I knew this relationship was messy and not what God ordained for my life. I was stuck and could not get out.

It's crazy how I picked up on his need for attention early during our relationship but had no idea it was signs of this disorder. Everywhere we went he had to be the attention of the room. It got so bad he would choose me to joke about in front of others just to make himself seem superior and extremely funny. People would be talking, and he would interrupt the conversation by reverting it back to him saying, "I did this, and I did that." Geesh!!!! Why does everything have to be about you? My goodness. All of the love, in the beginning, was just a blindfold to control the relationship. He was so secretive with everything, recalling why he didn't want any of my pictures on his social media and only took me around certain friends because he was living a double life, just in case something seemed better came along. Everything had to be so exclusive. Derrick told me once, "Everyone who needs to know about you, knows of you." I thought, Hmmmm!!! What does that really mean?

Once everything was revealed to me and tons of research was done on this disorder, I broke down and cried until I couldn't cry any longer again. In my secret place, my closet, I had to apologize to God for being upset and blaming him. When God said, "He was just saving my identity and saving my life I had no idea what it meant until after the fact." Literally, my life was saved because I was losing myself. I was giving more than I should, and it was changing me into someone else. Someone I never saw before. A person I was beginning not to recognize. Walking around like a zombie trying to make sure Derrick needs was met. My cry out to God completely changed from God, "Why did you remove him from my life to God thank you for keeping me, even when I didn't want to be kept. Thank you for your grace and mercy. Thank you for your protection over my life. God, thank you for saving my identity." Asking God, "How did I allow this to happen for so long? I knew things were wrong but could not get out, I was stuck. Crying out, "God, you are so worthy, thank you for saving my life. Your love is sufficient, and your love is unconditional." Tears rolling nonstop because I could have been dead, but God kept me.

God allowed Derrick to walk out of my life because I was supposed to leave two years before this happened but didn't. I was disobedient to what God told me to do. I did what I wanted to. So because I ignored the voice of God, he removed Derrick because I didn't have the strength to do on my own.

CHAPTER 21

Rebuilding In My Brokenness To Make Me Whole Again

Irealized there was one common denominator in these relationships and that was me. Asking God, "Why God? What is wrong with me? Feeling rejected and unworthy. It seems as though I'm attracting the same type people in my life and I don't understand what it is I'm doing wrong. I'm giving my love but taken advantage of, giving and it was never enough. Spending so much time in that secret place, I was led to the word of God, Psalm 118. Reading certain scriptures of Psalm 118, read like this, "O give thanks unto the Lord, for he is good because his mercy endures forever. I called upon the Lord in distress, and he answered, and set me in a high place. It is better to trust in the Lord than to put confidence in man. O give thanks unto the Lord, for he is good and his mercy endures forever.

God reminded me I was putting my trust in the wrong people. To follow him and he would always direct my path. God brought to my attention I was broken since my early childhood years when my parents got a divorce. Being separated from my father caused trauma in my life. Once the divorce of my parents, my mother brought my sister and me to Florida. My dad went to New York, and a part of me died. I missed my father very much. From that point in my life, I looked for love in all the wrong places. Craving for the love I lost when my father left. Tears flowing, yes I know this is deep right? But how could I know this if God didn't reveal it to me? When I was forced to be separated from my father at an early age, losing contact with him, I have always craved and desperately searched for the attention and love of a man. The love I was missing from my father.

There was a void in my life that a man was supposed to fill, at least that is what I expected. I didn't look to God to fill that void. I expected my significant other to fill that void missing from the love of my father. The void could never be filled because it wasn't their responsibility to fill it. I should have learned to love myself first. If I were in love with myself and realized the value of me, no way in this lifetime, I would have allowed myself to go through the things I went through in each relationship. I so desperately needed to feel loved and settled for whatever love or so-called love I was getting at the time.

Love turned into pain, addicted to the pain. I got used to the pain and rejection. I got used to failing relationships to the point a little love and attention was better than nothing at all. Settled and broken is where I was in life. Feeling empty and lonely. Turning to alcohol trying to fill that void only to get that temporary fix until the drunkenness wore off. Trust me I paid for it all the next day. Going through all of this and still empty on the inside.

God forced me to realize it was time to be removed from this vicious and revolving cycle. I was broken all the way down to the fact of wanting to take my life because the pain was unbearable and I was definitely tired. God said, "I broke you all the way down to rebuild you again. To make you realize your true value and make you whole again. Some people were only in your life for a season, and you had a hard time of letting people go. Everyone cannot go where I'm taking you. You have to be really careful as to who you attach yourself to. People desperately want to destroy what I have instilled in you. I am rebuilding you and taking you to higher heights. Many that didn't believe in you will eventually see the glory of God in your life".

Tears were continually rolling down my face, but tears of joy. The tears were because of finally having peace in my life. I'm at peace in my life after almost 40 years of living. I was lost in the shuffle and couldn't get out. The cycle has definitely been broken. In the word of God, Philippians 4:7, it says, "And the peace of God, which passeth all understanding, if you keep your hearts and minds stayed on Christ Jesus." I cannot even explain the peace I have in my life. It is like a sense of calmness, knowing that whatever battle comes my way, God got me.

I have learned to love my children and myself unconditionally. If people don't meet the expectation of God, they have no place here. He is my peace, my provider, my protector, and my leader, guiding me through this thing we call life. God never promised there would not be trials and tribulations. But he did promise to keep you in perfect peace and to be your protector. Looking at things so differently now about life. No longer will I stoop to people and their level in life. No longer will I allow people to take advantage of me as a human being. No longer will I allow people to control my destiny. I am free. I am free from bondage. While writing this book I just want to run and scream because no one has me at this point in my life but the Lord Jesus Christ. I prayed my way through the brokenness of my life. God had me at a place that I could depend on no one but him. In the famous voice of Bishop TD Jakes, "When people can walk away from you let them walk. Don't talk another person into staying in your life. Your destiny is never tied to any person that left. People leave you because they're not joined to you. Let them go! You have to know when people part in your story is over. Let them walk!" Do you know there is healing and deliverance in your brokenness? I am much stronger and wiser now. If anyone asks me how I got through it? My answer to you, "It was God."

Since my brokenness, God has blessed me tremendously, look he gave me provision to write this book, and I did it. My business called, "Country Girl Soul-food and Seafood LLC" is growing. It's not where it should be, but God said, "He is taking me to higher heights" so that means the increase is coming, patience is vital. My children are happy and do not want for anything. The relationship with their father, Darius has changed tremendously for the better. No matter what anyone says, children need their father. Please keep that in mind when parents are fighting about something that has nothing to do with your children. They still need both parents. This is extremely important.

I also have a grandson that was born. His name is Carter. He is such a cutie and bundle of joy. Cater reminds me so much of my son when he was born. They look just alike. It's definitely like raising my son all over again, and I love it. I'm at peace in my life and this feeling I would not change for the world. It was no one but God's grace that has changed my life. Things that used to bother me don't bother me any longer.

Always remember when going through please trust the process. No matter how much it hurts, trust the process. God will never leave you or forsake you. Only he knows what is planned for your life and the destiny he has for you. Never allow another person to control your destiny. With God all things are possible. The only validation you need is from God and no one else but him. Please stay encouraged and be blessed.

58812672R00095

Made in the USA
Columbia, SC
25 May 2019